TAKE MY LIFE

TAKE
MY
LIFE

MICHAEL GRIFFITHS

Inter-Varsity Fellowship
39 Bedford Square, London WC1

© Inter-Varsity Fellowship

First edition January 1967
Reprinted May 1967

Printed in Great Britain by
Hazell Watson & Viney Ltd,
Aylesbury, Bucks

CONTENTS

FOREWORD

'The Importance of Not Being Earnest'

It is today a common idea that to be adult and mature you should not be too enthusiastic about anything; or that if you should happen to be enthusiastic, then it should be very carefully concealed beneath a mask of careless superficiality. The only thing worse than earnestness is fanaticism, particularly religious fanaticism. In society at large a Christian with a sense of dedicated mission is a rare and unpopular, even slightly ridiculous, figure. The trend of our times is to minimize differences, while the mass media condition us to conformity in diet, dentifrice, dress and denominational convictions. Worldly common sense dictates moderation in all things. 'We should be tolerant of each other. Why be so ill-mannered as to insist on being different, or so bigoted as to believe that you are right and others wrong?'

There is still some idealism among students who are willing to espouse a cause and make it so much their own that they will brave hardship, ridicule and arrest in order to forward their aims. Whether they sit on pavements in Britain, sing 'We will overcome' in the United States, or snake-march in Japan—they are ready to take positive action for what they believe. They petition names outside stations, hold open-air meetings, march in demonstrations, sit down in defiance of police batons, tear-gas and arrest. But that is quite different from religion, of course.

Christians seem a tame, insipid lot by comparison. You cannot get very worked up about institutional Christianity—at least, not in favour of it. Religion does not seem to have very much urgency about it. It is not at all contemporary and is apparently concerned primarily with the upkeep of old buildings, collecting money for organs, and preserving the antiquarian relics of a former generation. It has its own special smell of musty pews and prayer books. It has its own special language, much of it at least three centuries out of date, some of it older still. Religion is suspect of being, if not frankly superstitious, at least sentimental and escapist. For the world's problems of suffering and injustice it seems to offer pious platitudes, an occasional resolution, but no action. There is apparently no 'great leap forward' planned by the Christian church, and the prospect of there ever being one looks increasingly remote. Being a Christian seems at best rather pedestrian, if not completely static, and at worst anti-progressive.

Oliver Wendell Holmes is reported to have said: 'In my heart there is a plant called Reverence and it needs watering about once a week.' Christianity has become identified with a stereotyped performance held once or so each week, and attended only by the pious few interested enough to attend. If it were not for christenings, marriages and funerals, one wonders if the whole thing would not just fold up. Small wonder that to be a 'Christian' seems rather dull and ordinary, and has little appeal to the vast mass of people.

The word 'Christianity' is never found in the Bible, and the word 'Christian' which does occur seems to describe something quite different from what we call by that name now. Are we present-day Christians just a lot of phoneys who do not believe what we say we believe? A great deal has been written recently about people's image of what God is like. The popular image of what a Christian ought to be like seems to have suffered also, even

inside the churches themselves. The aim of this little
book is to make us rethink what it means to be a Christian
—one of Christ's men—in the Bible meaning of the word.
Clearly it involves much more than an hour a week of
passive attendance in a building set apart for religious
worship, watching a performance given by a theologically
trained professional, listening to a short homily, and
dropping a few coins into a bag passed around for the
purpose.

The modern virtues of toleration and moderation seem
to find little place in the Bible. There seems to be an all-
or-nothingness about the things that Christ told His
disciples to do. Being a Christian is set out as being
something living and dynamic; he is somebody with a
passionate vitality and joy in living. This book is a plea
for action—for a return to a Bible-conditioned type of
Christian and a New Testament-conditioned kind of
church. No book can stir us to action—the Holy Spirit of
God alone can do that. That is why each chapter ends
in the way it does, for this is a book about a Christian's
eager response to God, in a joyous spontaneity of service
for Him and for all mankind. Amy Carmichael used to
ask for 'fire words' and for books with 'blood and iron' in
them. The Bible is such a book. Whether this book will
be I don't know, but I do know that we want 'blood and
iron' type Christians.

Tokyo   MICHAEL GRIFFITHS
October 1965

1 BALANCE or FANATICISM?

Take my heart, it is Thine own;
It shall be Thy royal throne.

Talking about 'full surrender' to Christ makes some people feel uncomfortable. 'This consecration business can be overdone and it's easy to take things too far. Surely Christianity does not make wild demands upon us to become religious fanatics. We have to be practical and sensible—"moderation in all things", you know. Isn't that what the Bible says?'

I remember being gently teased by a fellow missionary: 'Ah, I can see that you were in the IVF; they specialize in being balanced, don't they?' Certainly most of us are in favour of balance and moderation: we must by all means avoid going to extremes. As Christians, however, we need above all to be biblical and our much-vaunted balance and moderation may become, as we must admit if we are honest, a very convenient cloak for compromise, half-heartedness and sloth.

It may not be helpful, therefore, to rush straight into a discussion of the need to be disciplined in our use of time and money, and the need to dedicate all we have to God, for this may frighten some people off altogether, while the rest of us will invoke the blessed category of balance and moderation, and that will be that. First of all, then, we have to see whether the Bible encourages wild-eyed fanaticism or whether the Bible pattern for living is wholesome, sane, winsome and utterly reasonable.

11

We need to remember also that this is no mere academic, impersonal discussion. We are talking about God. This God is real and He wants to have a real relationship with us. Immediately we become cautious; let's be moderate and not commit ourselves to anything. Just as some men shy away from marriage when they suddenly realize what it involves, so people shy away when they realize suddenly that being a Christian involves a relationship with—and no printed words can convey the awe and wonder that ought to be in our voices when we say the last word of this sentence—with God. Is it possible, then, that our Creator, our heavenly Father, our Saviour God, our merciful Friend could make unreasonable or unwholesome demands upon us? Perish the thought! If we cannot trust Him, whom *can* we trust? Clearly, then, first of all we have to think about the grounds upon which any appeal for Christian action, moderate or not so moderate, must be based.

The Bible itself says very little commending moderation. Does the Bible anywhere suggest that we are to be moderately good, moderately holy, moderately zealous? Or does it anywhere permit us to be just moderately selfish and moderately self-indulgent? To suggest this would be a travesty of what the Bible teaches. The history of the Old Testament might be described as the history of a people who wanted to be moderate and tolerant in their religion, and of how God would not permit this. He is continually rebuking them and persistently calling them to fanatical holiness, social justice, religious intolerance and enthusiastic righteousness. When, in spite of repeated warnings, they stubbornly fail to separate themselves from compromise with idolatry, social injustice and unholy living, He judges them and chastens them.

Several misquotations

But whatever the Old Testament says, surely the New
Testament takes a much more reasonable and tolerant
attitude? After all, it is Paul who says, 'Let your moderation be known unto all men' (Phil. 4: 5, AV).[1] What does
'moderation' mean? (*The Concise Oxford Dictionary*
doesn't give you much help, for it reads, 'Moderation, n.
Moderating; moderateness; *in* —, in a moderate manner
or degree.') It means not going to extremes, the opposite
of going to excess. Yes, but is that what the Bible means?
Lightfoot[2] calls it a 'gentle and forbearing spirit', 'for-
bearance' being the opposite to a spirit of contention and
self-seeking. The Greek word *epieikēs* is, in fact, a word
meaning 'yielding, gentle, kind', and it is translated as
'gentle' in 1 Timothy 3: 3; Titus 3: 2; James 3: 17; 1
Peter 2: 18. 'Moderation', then, is just a bad translation!

But common sense would also suggest that it is unwise
to try to use a text from Philippians to advocate half-
heartedness! Look at the rest of the letter! It speaks of
Jesus Christ as One who went to extreme lengths to save
men, to the extent of taking the form of a slave (2: 6, 7)
and suffering the humiliation and utter loss of face involved in dying as a convicted fraud and deceiver. Paul
himself speaks of his own readiness to be poured out as
a libation upon the sacrificial offering of the Philippians'
faith (2: 17). He speaks quite immoderately about what it
means to be a follower of Christ: 'to live is Christ, and
to die is gain' (1: 21). 'For his sake I have suffered the loss
of all things' (3: 8). These ideas scarcely encourage 'moderation' in matters of faith. It emerges, then, that this
verse does not bear the meaning which is sometimes put

[1] Biblical quotations are taken from the Revised Standard Version
(1946–52), unless otherwise stated, as here.
[2] J. B. Lightfoot, *Philippians* (Macmillan, 1878; Oliphants, 1953),
p. 158.

upon it: the Bible in fact nowhere teaches moderation (in this sense at any rate).

We can understand this by making a few misquotations from the same letter, illustrating the interesting fact that biblical statements are only extremely rarely qualified or limited; they are almost always absolute statements without any qualification to weaken their force. Paul does not pray for the Philippians that their love may abound within reason, with some measure of knowledge and discernment, so that they may give qualified approval to that which is excellent, and may be moderately pure and by and large blameless for the day of Christ, being half filled with the fruits of righteousness (see Phil. 1: 9–11). Neither, later, does he want them to be moderately blameless and by and large innocent, children of God without many obvious blemishes in the midst of a somewhat crooked and slightly perverse generation, among whom they glimmer feebly like glowworms in the dusk (see Phil. 2: 15).

The kind of rejoicing and exultant faith in the Lord, about which Paul is writing, comes from unqualified obedience to absolute commands, stemming from an utterly whole-hearted allegiance to a God whom he can portray only by piling up superlatives upon superlatives. Such a God, by His very character, cannot be satisfied with qualified support, conditional obedience or relative sanctity. Only the very best is good enough for Him.

Did Jesus teach moderation?

There is a remarkable all-or-nothing quality about the claims and commands of Christ. They are starkly, almost frighteningly, absolute statements or demands, without qualifying clauses or exceptions. (So much so that Bishop Charles Gore wanted to make the famous Matthean exception, 'except for fornication' in Matthew 19: 9, an interpolation rather than a genuine saying of Jesus, in spite of the absence of any textual evidence to support the contention!)

Just consider some of the things that Christ said. Some of them we shall naturally be referring to in more detail later in the book, but take, just for example, the ideas of following Jesus, of obeying God's word and of giving to God.

Following Jesus

Jesus often called men to follow Him. The first disciples, Peter and Andrew, were commanded: ' "Follow me, and I will make you fishers of men." Immediately they left their nets and followed him. And going on from there he saw two other brothers, James the son of Zebedee and John his brother, in the boat with Zebedee their father, mending their nets, and he called them. Immediately they left the boat and their father, and followed him' (Mt. 4: 18–22). We are not told what their father thought about it, left to run the family business without the help of his two sons. There is no mention of any discussion of conditions of service; just that they were called and they went.

On a later occasion a man who vowed to follow Jesus everywhere was made to reconsider his attitude, presumably because he was not really prepared to follow unconditionally; while another who tried to delay his actual break with home was told to follow at once (Mt. 8: 19–22). Nothing is to be allowed to hinder obedience to Christ's call.

Matthew himself just got up and left his office when he was called. There was no discussion about whether he would get a pension for a premature retirement, about delay pending the appointment of a successor, or about how he would be supported financially from now on. 'Follow me,' said Jesus, and Matthew did just that (Mt. 9: 9).

This following is a totalitarian business. Jesus must be

loved more than father or mother, more than son or daughter (and for most of us these relationships are the most precious and demanding of all), and 'he who does not take his cross and follow me is not worthy of me' (Mt. 10: 38). There is nothing very 'moderate' about this. Nobody honestly reading such passages as this could suggest that it means that we are to be 'moderate' about following Christ. Peter, ever given to straightforwardness, said, 'Lo, we have left everything and followed you.' Following Jesus is to be a whole-hearted business and all other things take second place. There is no suggestion anywhere in the New Testament that we may practise moderation in the degree in which we follow Jesus.

Obeying God's word

In the Sermon on the Mount Jesus speaks severely about those who relax the commands of God or who teach men so. The law is to be obeyed (Mt. 5: 17–21). What matters is not outwardly impressive words, 'Lord, Lord,' nor outwardly impressive deeds of prophecy, exorcism and the like, but doing 'the will of my Father who is in heaven'. The wise man is the one who hears these words and does them (Mt. 7: 21–27). There is no suggestion here of moderation. It is a scrupulous and full-orbed obedience which the Lord commands. It is worth noting that the Sermon on the Mount is not just a lot of good ethical advice or encouragement to moral behaviour, but contains definite commands about whole-hearted obedience. Later the Lord Jesus warns that we must answer in the day of judgment 'for every careless word' (Mt. 12: 36). There is no suggestion that a 50% pass mark will do where words are concerned.

In Luke's Gospel (6: 46), in the same context of building on the rock, Jesus says: 'Why do you call me "Lord, Lord," and not do what I tell you?' It is a striking challenge to face up to the implications of Christ being one's

Lord; it means that obedience is expected. A reasonable modicum of obedience is not considered sufficient.

The pious woman who makes a sanctimonious remark about the blessing of being the mother of Jesus receives the sharp rejoinder: 'Blessed rather are those who hear the word of God and keep it!' (Lk. 11: 28). To Jesus nothing matters like obedience. It is very difficult to see how one can advocate only moderate adherence to the commands of God and remain true to what is written in the Bible. Moderate obedience is a euphemism for disobedience.

Giving to God

What could be more fanatical than the action of the poor widow who gave her last two coins to the temple treasury for the service of God (Lk. 21: 2)? Yet her giving is commended, for 'she out of her poverty put in all the living that she had'.

Or there is the other woman (Mt. 26: 7), identified as Mary the sister of Martha (Jn. 12: 3ff.), who broke open the alabaster box full of precious ointment and anointed Him with it. Though this was regarded as a piece of extravagance by others, the Lord defended her: 'She has done a beautiful thing . . . Wherever this gospel is preached in the whole world, what she has done will be told in memory of her.' It was the fragrance of this immoderate giving which filled the house. Sometimes when we read this story we are embarrassed by this woman, and feel we want to look the other way. Yet this is the kind of whole-hearted devotion to Christ which the Gospel commends to us.

Balance

Does this mean, then, that moderation is not a biblical virtue at all, and that we are expected to be fanatical about being a Christian? In a certain sense I think it does! There is a wonderful balance about the teaching of the Bible. But the qualifications do not appear as exceptions or modifications of the absolute principles laid down. The commands and principles do in fact qualify each other; not in such a way as to weaken their absolute force, but in such a way as to deepen our understanding of how they should be applied. Let us look at three examples of this interplay of the absolute principles and commands laid down in the Bible.

1. 'Do not lay up for yourselves treasures on earth, . . . but . . . in heaven' (Mt. 6: 19). Now this clear principle is qualified in one sense by the injunction, 'If any one does not provide for his relatives, and especially for his own family, he has disowned the faith and is worse than an unbeliever' (1 Tim. 5: 8). This second principle prevents us understanding the command as meaning that we should not accumulate *any* capital or make any deposit in the bank. But in fact helping our relatives and dependants may be a costly and sacrificial business, and by doing this I shall be laying up treasure in heaven, so that the principle is not abrogated. I may have to lay up some treasure on earth in order to support my dependants, though I shall have to take care that I do not lay aside more than is needed for that purpose, nor ignore the beggar who may be lying at my gate. The principles, then, qualify each other only in the sense that they prevent us from misapplying or distorting them. It is not a matter of taking moderate care of one's dependants and laying up a moderate amount of treasure in heaven. Both the injunctions continue to apply.

2. 'Humble yourselves therefore under the mighty hand of God' (1 Pet. 5: 6). Here is an absolute principle. We are nowhere urged to be moderately humble and to avoid going to extremes in humility. There is an interesting example of how a virtue like humility can be distorted in the book *The Nun's Story*.[3] The nun heroine, a doc-

[3] Kathryn Hulme, *The Nun's Story* (Muller, 1956).

18

tor's daughter with considerable intelligence and nursing ability, is suspected of needing something to abase her pride in her abilities. It is suggested to her that she should deliberately fail her exams in Tropical Medicine as an 'act of humility', for others will imagine that her failure arises from stupidity or laziness. She has a tremendous inner struggle: is it God's will that she should fail? Is it just intellectual pride that makes her reluctant to write down wrong answers? In the event she cannot dissemble and she passes out near the top of the list. Does it mean that she was unwilling to surrender her intellectual pride, and that she wanted to be only moderately humble? It would undoubtedly have done her good to fail, to have her intellectual pride humbled. But there were other biblical principles involved here. There was personal integrity, for to write down answers known to be false would be a form of false witness. Secondly, a Christian should be diligent and do everything whole-heartedly to the glory of God. Thirdly, there is the question of the time and the money spent on the course, and a proper stewardship of them for God. The method of reaching a humble frame of mind suggested to her was impossible without infringing other Christian principles.

3. 'You shall love the Lord your God with all your heart, and with all your soul, and with all your mind' (Mt. 22: 37). It is quite obvious that loving God like this does not mean that we shall therefore have no love left for anyone else! Even though the 'all' is quite absolute and inclusive, loving God like this does not exclude loving your neighbour as yourself, the command which follows in the succeeding verse. Nobody can excuse himself for not loving his neighbour on the grounds that he is far too busy loving God! (Though presumably it was some casuistry of this kind that was in the mind of those who ignored the wounded man lying by the road, who was later helped by the good Samaritan.) That a man loves his wife with all his heart does not exclude his loving the

child that she bears him. This love, moreover, is extensible to include additional children, without diminishing one whit his love for the wife and the first child. It is not a question of reducing love to one's wife, first to 50%, and then to $33\frac{1}{3}$%, and so on! Loving our fellow-men and loving God at the same time does not mean that we must love God moderately (say 50%) and our neighbours moderately (25%) on a par with loving oneself (the other 25%)! Obeying the command to love our neighbours is going to be one of the ways in which we demonstrate our love for God.

Balance, then, is not a matter of mathematical proportion, giving proportional attention to various biblical principles, say 25% to this, 35% to that and 40% to this. The principles are all to be observed 100% simultaneously. There is no room for being moderate in one's loyalty and obedience to Jesus Christ.

Fanaticism

'Fanatic' is a scare-word, like Methodist, Pietist, Enthusiast, Fundamentalist, and so on. We use it to pillory single-minded whole-heartedness. The word conjures up a vision of some wild-eyed, gesticulating ascetic armed with an enormous Bible, somebody who is queer, odd, eccentric, who takes up an odd and extreme position about everything. The word sometimes tells something about the people who use it, for someone has defined a fanatic as 'a person inspired by excess of zeal, if that person is in the presence of other persons who are not in like manner inspired by excess of zeal'. This may be so, but one does meet such people; they are fanatics, and there is no other word for them.

What makes such a person so offensive? It may be that they are ostentatious, inconsiderate, ill-mannered, overbearing, narrow-minded, self-opinionated under the cover of religion, and so on. But these offensive things do not arise because the man is being too biblical and is carrying his Christianity to absurd lengths, so much as because the man is not biblical enough! You cannot take Christianity 'too far', if you apply it properly. The truly biblical man may make us feel uncomfortable, yet he has a winsomeness and attractiveness about him that reminds us of Christ Himself. If the man is offensively 'fanatical' it is not because he follows the Bible 'to the letter', but rather because he is failing to observe some crucial biblical principles, and emphasizing some at the expense of others. It is not so much that he is failing to be moderate, but that he is failing to be equally 'fanatical' about all the teaching of Christ: the strong warnings about ostentation in Matthew 6, for example. He may need to become 'fanatically' considerate for other people and 'fanatically' humble! The Bible commands separation from worldliness (and we should be fanatical about this in the full biblical sense of the fleshly and carnal mind, rather than merely abstaining from habits and customs which tend to vary from country to country), but this does not mean that the Christian is to have no contacts with non-Christians apart from preaching judgment to them. (2 Cor. 6: 17ff. needs to be read in the light of 1 Cor. 5: 10.) We are to walk as He walked (1 Jn. 2: 6), who was the friend of publicans and sinners. The offensive element, then, in fanaticism arises from a failure to be fully biblical and like the Lord Jesus. Such people are, in a literal sense, eccentric, like a wheel not properly centred, more fanatical about some Christian truths than others. It is not that such people need to become more moderate, but rather more 'fanatical' in obeying every command of Christ and not just some of them. The Lord Jesus Himself was utterly whole-hearted, but this attracted men and did not repel them.

We need, therefore, not to become more moderate, but more diligent, studying our Bibles to find out just what

God's commandments are, so that we may call Him Lord and do the things which He says. His command to 'Go . . . and make disciples of all nations, baptizing them . . .' continues 'teaching them to observe *all* that I have commanded you' (Mt. 28: 19), suggesting that what we must teach is an absolute and all-round, full-orbed obedience to the teaching of Jesus Christ. Only so shall we avoid the Scylla of a tepid moderation, a diluted Christianity, on the one hand and the Charybdis of a distorted and eccentric, one-track fanaticism on the other.

So often, too, when we oppose moderation to fanaticism, what we are really advocating is sloth rather than diligence, and compromise rather than obedience. Sloth was once included in the Seven Deadly Sins but is too near a relation to moderation and tolerance to be rudely spoken of these days. We shun people for some sins against society, and in some circles the man who drinks or smokes, but we have yet to hear of the man who is avoided for being slothful and lazy. Rather inconsistent, isn't it?

Did Jesus practise moderation?

The Jesus of the Gospels is the great Nonconformist. Even a very cursory reading makes it plain that Jesus was always being criticized for His failure to conform to the expected pattern. He was, in the opinion of the people of His day, extremely unconventional. Why does He hobnob with the riff-raff and disreputable people (Mk. 2: 16)? Why do they feast instead of fasting (2: 18)? Why are they so casual about keeping the details of the Law (2: 24)? He had answers for all these questions, but neither His answers nor His reasons seem always to have been understood.

He was accused not only of being unconventional, but also of being a fanatic. They did not use that word, but the words they used were intended to wound and hurt. They said that He was possessed by Beelzebub and cast out demons through the prince of demons (Mk. 3: 22). He has a demon and is mad (Jn. 10: 20). He is a Samaritan and demon-possessed (Jn. 8: 48). He was a greedy fellow, fond of the wine cup and a friend of the riff-raff (Lk. 7: 34). It seems that He was not moderate. He was not the kind of colourless character about whom nobody has any bad word to say, or good word either. He was not out to please people by compromising in order to avoid offence. He insisted that the new wine of the new covenant could not be contained in the old legalistic bottles; the accepted forms were inadequate and unable to serve the new kingdom.

He seems to have been rather an uncomfortable person to be with, but when He differs from the customs of His time we can see that He is right to differ, and that it is our thinking which has been wrong. There is a perfection and an order and a sanity about all that He says and does. Here is One who does all things well, who is full of grace and truth, and out of whose mouth proceed gracious words, and indeed nobody else ever spoke as wonderfully as He spoke (Mk. 7: 37; Jn. 1: 14; Lk. 4: 22; Jn. 7: 46). His claims seem to be extreme and absolute, and the authority He claims is supreme. His own dedication is to finish the work (Jn. 4: 34; 5: 36) which His Father has given Him to do, and His meat and drink is to do the will of God. He has a tremendous sense of being hemmed in, constrained (Lk. 12: 50), until it is accomplished. Here is a man with His face steadfastly set to go to Jerusalem (Lk. 9: 51), so much so that those who followed were frightened by the intensity of His purpose (Mk. 10: 32ff.). Is this an attitude of moderation, of not taking things too far? Here is One in Gethsemane, calling on God with strong crying and tears (Heb. 5: 7, AV), going on to death, even the shameful death of the cross. Is this moderation?

It is the theme of this book that being a Christian calls

for this same single-minded devotion to the will of God. It is not enough that we add a few religious exercises to our busy programme, that we water the plant of reverence once a week. There is to be, in a wholesome and gloriously sane biblical sense, a readiness to be thought fanatical— if that word is taken as the opposite of slothful, half-hearted moderation and easy-going religious mediocrity. The Christian is not to seek to be eccentric or to cultivate behaviour which attracts attention to himself; but there are occasions when his Christian testimony will have to be made in utter disregard of the smiles, sneers, hostility or social ostracism which he fears it may bring upon him. The charge of being a 'fanatic' should not deter us, provided we are beside ourselves (2 Cor. 5: 13) only in a biblical sense. None of us wants to make a spectacle of ourselves (1 Cor. 4: 9) before men. None of us likes seeming to be ridiculous in the eyes of others. Most of us would rather conform if we can, and to be a fool, even for Christ's sake (1 Cor. 4: 10), does not appeal to us very much. Many of us, round the cheerful fire in the comradeship of the moment, are tempted like Peter: we hesitate to identify ourselves with the despised and rejected Jesus, the bloody welts on His back and the spittle on His cheeks. For there is a challenge in the cross, as well as healing and blessing and forgiveness. Simply this, that if Jesus did all this for you, is anything too much for you to do for Him?

We are afraid to be thought fools or fanatics. But there are times when, if we are to be faithful to the Lord Jesus, we must risk it. That is the theme of this book.

It is easy to read and acknowledge truths intellectually, or to recognize failure theoretically, without taking any corresponding spiritual action. Each chapter of this book therefore ends with suggestions for private prayer.

Suggestions for prayer and meditation

Have I been guilty of describing compromise as balance, and concealing sloth as moderation? What am I going to do about it?

How far am I committed to Jesus Christ to obey Him as my Lord, and am I really prepared to accept the sovereign authority of His claims on my life?

Is there a need to dedicate my life afresh to the Lord Jesus now, with a prayer of repentance and renewed trust?

Is my enthusiasm for the service of Christ cooling with the years?

Is it just that I have become more balanced and mature, or was I more whole-hearted and warmer in my faith then than now?

'I know your works: you are neither cold nor hot. Would that you were cold or hot! So, because you are lukewarm, and neither cold nor hot, I will spew you out of my mouth' (Rev. 3: 15, 16).

'There is no coldness, Lord, in Thee,
  O keep us kindled, lest we bring
To our dear Lord of Calvary
  Dead ashes for our offering.'

AMY CARMICHAEL

2

FREEDOM
or SLAVERY?

Take my will, and make it Thine;
It shall be no longer mine.

Evangelistic appeals are sometimes couched in such terms as 'Will you serve and follow Christ?' We then mistakenly fall into the habit of mind of thinking that we are really doing God rather a favour by becoming a Christian. From this it is but a step to thinking that we will serve Christ just as much as we find convenient ('Life these days is so full') and can fit in with all the other things which we want to do.

The Christian, according to the Bible, is one who has become a slave of Jesus Christ. If we call Jesus 'Lord Jesus', then it implies that He is *my* Lord and that I am His slave. This idea of slavery or service is a very common one in the New Testament. The commonest word (Gk. *doulos*) means a slave, as opposed to a master or a free-man. The related verbs speak of the service performed by such a bondslave, that which he is bound to give to his master. The second most common noun (*diakonos*, from which the word deacon is derived) and its related verbs stress more the kind of work which the servant does rather than the relationship. The word is associated with waiting at table. There are other words used, among which the words for a household servant (*oikētēs*) and for steward (*oikonomos*), that is the household manager answerable to the master, are worth mentioning because the idea of Christian 'stewardship' is a common one to which we shall refer later.

The Christian is a slave

We may find the notion of being a slave rather offensive: '*I* don't want to be told what to do.' It sounds rather feudal and old-fashioned. The word is, however, used of the Lord Jesus Himself. In the letter to the Philippians (2: 7), the heavenly Lord (*kurios*) has taken on Him the form of a slave (*doulos*). He also uses of Himself the verb for waiting at table, when He says that He has not come to be ministered unto, but to minister (Mt. 20: 28). If we own Him as Lord (and we are not Christians at all unless we do, Rom. 10: 9), and if He who is our Lord was willing to become a slave and a waiter in order to serve us, how much more ought we to be willing to become His slaves, and to wait on Him. This relationship is implied whenever we talk of the *Lord* Jesus Christ. We have given Him our allegiance and become His servants. It is significant that, while the other words for servant are used literally of those whose profession is that of being a servant, it is the word for slave which is used metaphorically of the Christian to express his relationship to his Master.

A slave was the property of his master; his living body belonged to his master and he was not free till he was dead. He was not a hired man like the labourers in the vineyard, who were hired each day (Mt. 20: 1ff., Gk. *ergatēs*). He belonged absolutely to his master. This lights up the meaning of a passage like 1 Corinthians 6: 19, 20: 'You are not your own; you were bought with a price. So glorify God in your body.' Paul is saying that we have been purchased by God as slaves, we are no longer our own property. Our duty is to serve the Master who has purchased us for His service. In the following chapters, speaking really of social classes, he says again: 'Were you a slave when called? Never mind. But if you can gain your freedom, avail yourself of the opportunity. For he who was called in the Lord as a slave is a freedman of the Lord. Likewise he who was free when called is a slave of Christ' (1 Cor. 7: 21–24). That is to say, the man who may be socially a freedman is still a slave of Jesus Christ. Or again, in the well-known passage in Romans 6: 17–22, Paul says that his readers were once 'slaves of sin' (verse 17) but are now the slaves of righteousness (18), and then (in verse 22) he uses the verb and says that they have become enslaved to God. This idea brings out the striking force of the words we have quoted already from Matthew 20: 28: 'The Son of man came not to be served but to serve, and to give his life as a ransom for many.' The word ransom is the redemption price of a slave, so that we may paraphrase this verse: 'I have not come to be served, but to serve and to give my life to redeem slaves.' On the cross Jesus paid the ransom price to set us free from the bondage of sin, and so our allegiance is transferred to the One who has become our new Owner.

Here we must stop and put the question to ourselves: Whose slave am I? Do I recognize the Lord Jesus Christ as my Master? Can I say 'I am no longer my own, I belong to Him'? In Japan the idea of the lord and his loyal retainers is a familiar one found over and over again in history and literature. To become a Christian is to acknowledge Jesus as your sovereign Master, as King of kings and Lord of lords, and to confess oneself to be henceforth His purchased possession, His slave. This book goes on to speak of loyalty to Jesus and of obedience to Him, but this will all be quite pointless if you do not belong to Him. His demands will seem extreme, His commands will seem burdensome and our reaction will be one of resentment and rebellion—unless we have settled this basic matter first of all. Have you confessed Jesus as your own Lord?

The humility of the slave

We have as our supreme example a Lord who humbled Himself to be born as a helpless infant in a stable, with its strong ammoniacal smell of animal dung, and who lived as a provincial labourer in one of the smallest vassal kingdoms of the Roman Empire. He took the form of a slave. He humbled Himself even to the death of the cross, gasping for breath as the weight of His broken body had to be lifted up on the crucifying nails. The man who had claimed power and glory was put to death in weakness and shame. If our proud spirits shrink from humility, we remember that our Lord has gone before us. Here was no false gentility to keep Him from mingling with the common herd of men, no fastidiousness which made Him shrink from contact with the diseased outcasts of society.

He invites us to enter a relationship of lowly, humble service with Him. He uses the example of the toiling, burdened ox, stumbling in the shafts with a load too great to move. Come to Me, says the Lord Jesus; share a double yoke with Me, for My yoke is easy and My burden is light. What we can never do alone, we can do when harnessed with Him. 'Learn from me; for I am gentle and lowly in heart' (Mt. 11: 29). It is the humble, lowly Lord, who has made Himself a servant, who calls us to serve with Him. Though He is our Lord and we are His slaves, yet He is so lowly that He is ready to serve with us. His gentleness is referred to again in the following chapter in Matthew's Gospel, in a quotation from one of the Servant passages from Isaiah (and it is possibly this Old Testament conception which is also referred to in Phil. 2: 7: 'taking the form of *the* Servant'), when we are told that he will not break the bruised reed or quench the smoking flax. He will gently fan our smoking wicks until they kindle into a burning flame.

But the disciples of Christ are not naturally humble:

we have to learn this from Him. We are naturally proud, ambitious, and not ready to take the lower place. On the way to the upper room (Lk. 22: 24–27) the disciples are arguing about who is the greatest among them. Jesus tells them that Christian leadership is different. 'Let . . . the leader (be) as one who serves' (this is the word for 'to wait at table'; *i.e.*, the leader is to wait on the rest), and then at the table he says, 'I am among you as one who serves.' The occasion is, of course, the same as that in John 13: 1–16.

They came to the upper room on that evening with their feet hot and sweaty, with the dust of the roads coating feet and sandals. But there was nobody present to do the slave's work of washing their feet. It must have been obvious to all that feet were unwashed, for, reclining at the table in the manner of that time, with your head and your hands by the table, supporting yourself on one elbow, the feet of the others at the table were only just over your other shoulder. Anyone who has lived in hot climates knows the smell of unwashed feet! But if you had just been competing to see who was the most important, you were not going to step down and admit you were the junior present. There was a long, painful, smelly silence. . . . It is Jesus who gets up, stripping off His outer clothes, girding Himself with a towel to perform the menial task of washing the feet of His own disciples. There must have been an embarrassing silence as the water splashed in the basin and the Master knelt and washed dirty feet. That this One who is so pure and clean should humble Himself to wash off *my* dirt, to defile Himself with *my* uncleanness. His words to gruffly protesting Peter make it clear that this must be submitted to, for it prefigured the cross, when He was to take the sin and filthiness of all mankind upon His pure and holy heart. That He who is so great, so gloriously holy, should take this on Himself—this is humility. If we have been shrinking from being slaves, too proud to be slaves, we are utterly shamed to see what He did. 'If I then, your Lord and Teacher, have washed your feet, you also ought to wash one another's feet. For I have given you an example, that you also should do as I have done to you. Truly, truly, I say to you, a slave is not greater than his master . . .' In other words, I have become your slave—now you become slaves to others as well.

The Christian faith is a revolutionary faith. It demands a complete change of attitude. But in some revolutions the aim of the revolution is that those who have been underneath get on top, whereas in this one those who have been proud put themselves underneath! We live in a society where status is important. Each one of us likes to carve out some kind of niche of self-importance. The man on top tells the others what to do and they wait on him and hope to occupy his shoes one day. But Christ tells us that the man who is great in God's eyes is the man who is more concerned to clean the other man's shoes than to occupy them! It is no less easy for this to happen in the local church. Men, who have no status in the community at large, seek to establish themselves as the local 'pope' in the restricted assembly of the local church or chapel. Nothing can be more inimical to real fellowship than men struggling for pre-eminence and importance in a small church—or a large one.

Even student groups are not immune from this danger, and a strong-minded fifth-year student can pontificate like any pope. Strong leadership is good, but such men often fail to train successors, and there is a slump after they leave, or they may be succeeded by another strong-minded person who is doctrinally vague and leads the whole group off its true course. The test of good leadership is what happens afterwards. It is interesting that, in the New Testament, leaders of local churches always seem to be in the plural rather than the singular, with the notable and significant exception of Diotrephes (3 Jn. 9), who was out solely for personal prestige. It is not unknown for students to be rivals for leadership, even to the point of encouraging factions. Or a student passed over for leadership goes off in a huff and leaves the group —which all goes to prove that those who felt he or she was unsuitable were right! Such an immature Christian, unwilling to be led by another, would not have been suitable for leadership.

The mother of James and John (Mt. 20: 20ff.) was ambitious for her boys, and she longed that they might occupy positions of importance when Jesus came into power. No doubt James and John, who were usually in the little circle of three who sometimes went with the Lord when others were left behind, probably shared their mother's more naïvely expressed ambition. But Christian values are different. The Gentiles want to lord it over one another all the time. But Christian greatness is of a different kind, and Jesus their Lord will Himself be the great example of One who came to serve.

The loyalty of the slave

In his book *The Christian Mind*, Harry Blamires has an interesting passage [1] on loyalty, which he suggests is 'a sham virtue exploited to give a bogus moral flavour to amoral or immoral actions', and says that 'Loyalty may be said to be evil in the sense that if any action is defended on the grounds of loyalty alone, it is defended on no rational grounds at all'. In other words, in the sense in which it is often used, loyalty is not a Christian virtue at all. When people have to make a claim on the basis of loyalty it suggests that it is overruling some other obvious ethical principle: be loyal to the firm even if its practice is dishonest; be loyal to me and save my face; be loyal to your country even if it means behaving in a scurrilous fashion internationally; be loyal to your race even if it

[1] H. Blamires, *The Christian Mind* (SPCK, 1963), pp. 23, 24.

FREEDOM OR SLAVERY?

means exploiting other races in defiance of the command
to love one's neighbour. Integrity is a Christian virtue,
but blind loyalty is not.

This idea is especially interesting to someone who lives
in Japan, where loyalty has long been exalted as a virtue.
History and literature are full of stories about loyalty
unto death for one's lord, even when it cannot do him
much good because he is dead already. To a Westerner
it seems at one and the same time both noble and quix-
otic. To the thinking Christian it seems almost idolatrous
to give such loyalty, involving suicide very often and
revenge not infrequently, to a mere man, however exalted.
The reason behind this would seem to be that loyalty is
a Christian virtue only when it is loyalty to God Himself,
and then the ideas of worship, honour and obedience are
more commonly used. Blamires suggests that loyalty to a
man, a party, a country, a cause must stand or fall on
whether that man or party or country is in fact being just
and good at the point where loyalty is requested. If the
cause is just, then the call to loyalty is redundant, because
it merits support as being just and true. But when we are
speaking about God, we know that here is Someone who
is not just relatively good, but absolutely so. There may
be times when we face a trial of loyalty towards God, but
this boils down then to a matter of faith or trust in God,
so that loyalty may be regarded as a positive expression
of faith and trust in God.

The loyalty of Jesus was challenged by Satan at the
beginning, when he offered an easy escape from Calvary
'if you will fall down and worship me' (Mt. 4: 9, 10).
The Lord replied at once: 'Begone, Satan! for it is written, "You shall worship the Lord your God and him only
shall you serve." ' (The Greek word here is *latreuō*, meaning religious service.) But the loyalty of Jesus is seen also
in His daily living: 'I always do what is pleasing to him'
(that is, the Father) (Jn. 8: 29). It is seen supremely in

T.M.L.—2

33

Gethsemane, in the words 'not my will, but thine, be done' (Lk. 22 : 42).

This challenge of loyalty to God is put straight to the Christian: 'No one can serve two masters; for either he will hate the one and love the other, or he will be devoted to the one and despise the other. You cannot serve God and mammon' (Mt. 6: 24). Here it is the verb 'to be enslaved', *i.e.* you cannot be the slave of two men at once. This is even more obvious in Luke 16: 13 where the word used for 'servant' is the word for 'household servant'; you cannot belong to two households at once. That is the issue: do I belong to the Lord and His household or not?

This is seen clearly by the centurion: 'I say . . . to my slave, "Do this," and he does it' (Mt. 8: 9). He understands that Jesus has this supreme authority over all things. If Jesus is the Lord, then I must accept His authority absolutely. I am not in a position to pick and choose, to discriminate between what pleases me to obey and agree with and what displeases me. There must be an unquestioning loyalty to the plain commands of Jesus.

There will be times when there will be a conflict of loyalties between our proper family affection and loyalty to Christ (Mt. 10: 34–39). There is no doubt which is to be the higher loyalty. He claims precedence over our nearest and dearest. As we have seen, it will normally be true that by loving them and pleasing them we shall be pleasing God; but there may be occasions when there is a conflict, especially if those we love best are not yet Christians. We may face conflicts over marriage with an unbeliever, over priority in use of holiday time or in the spending of money for self-indulgence.

This conflict occurs with other relationships. There is often a clear issue over the use of Sunday: shall it be participation in that trial match, revision for an examination or attendance at church? Which has priority? Or it may be a choice between a Christian camp, to give others a good holiday, and going off alone on some expensive continental trip. Or between sticking to one's academic work and fraternizing with some time-wasting clique in the Students' Union. Or a choice between dating a non-Christian boy or girl and attending the church young people's Bible Study. Christ demands precedence over all other claims. A choice between the good and the better is always more difficult than a straight choice between good and evil.

The self-denial of the slave

'If any man would come after me, let him deny himself and take up his cross daily and follow me. For whoever would save his life will lose it; and whoever loses his life for my sake, he will save it. For what does it profit a man if he gains the whole world and loses or forfeits himself?' (Lk. 9: 23–25).

What is our attitude towards ourselves and our lives? Are we really concerned only for our own self-indulgence and comfort, wanting to remain in sheltered security, refusing to hazard our lives? Or is it, for us, Jesus first and Jesus only? If this means going to live and work in places where there is a risk to health or to life—so be it. If it means turning one's back on favourite foods, valued amenities, the opportunity for sports and entertainments, even on beloved relatives and friends—so be it. The man who clings to these things, who wants to 'save his life', only stands to lose it. Most of us have a deep-seated fear of missing something, the best things, in life.

This fear is recognized in the Old Testament in an interesting passage where people were weeded out before battle (Dt. 20: 5–7). The officers were to ask, Who has built a new house and not dedicated it? Let him go home, lest he die in the battle and another man dedicate it. Who has planted a vineyard but has still to taste its fruit?

35

Let him go home, lest he die in the battle and somebody else eat it. Who is there who has been betrothed to a girl but has not yet married her? Let him go home, lest he be killed in the battle and some other fellow get her instead. These are deep-seated fears in many of us, and the Israelites recognized that a man with these things on his mind would be more interested in saving his own skin than fighting the battles of the Lord. Better send him away from the battle than have a half-hearted person who might turn and run and so discourage the rest.

But, significantly, these three features are mentioned again in the terrible section of cursings on those who break God's covenant, following the promises of blessing to those who keep the covenant of God, where it is said: 'You shall betroth a wife, and another man shall lie with her; you shall build a house, and you shall not dwell in it; you shall plant a vineyard, and you shall not use the fruit of it' (Dt. 28: 30). In other words, the man who tries to save his life will lose it, and all the things he has been trying to hold on to. He has turned his back on the Lord in order to hold on to these other things, and then he finds that that which he fears happens to him after all. Will he seek first the kingdom of God and His righteousness (Mt. 6: 33), or will he seek first these other things? Seek Christ first, and 'all these things shall be yours as well'. It may well be this Old Testament idea which lies at the back of the excuses offered by those invited to the banquet, who asked to be excused because of the land one had bought, the oxen another had bought and the new wife another had married (Lk. 14: 18–20).

Jesus asks that we deny ourselves, and this may well mean steeling ourselves for the unpleasant task. The hospital nuns in Kathryn Hulme's *Nun's Story* show that, whatever our doctrinal disapproval of religous orders, there is a truly biblical spirit at this point: 'All for Jesus, Sister William had said in the ward, pulling on the rubber gloves. Say it, my dear students, every time you are called upon for what seems an impossible task. Then you can do anything with serenity. It is a talisman phrase that takes away the disagreeable inherent in many nursing duties. Say it for the bedpans you carry, for the old incontinents you bathe, for those sputum cups of the tubercular. *Tout pour Jésus,* she said briskly, as she bent to change the dressing foul with corruption.'

This is what it may mean to deny oneself, and take up one's cross to follow Him. The slave has no rights; he is called to serve diligently and to go on serving. It does not matter if he is weary, or sick, or has worries of his own; his task is to get on with his work. This point is made very clearly in Luke 17: 7–10: 'Will any one of you, who has a servant (slave) plowing or keeping sheep, say to him when he has come in from the field, "Come at once and sit down at table"? Will he not rather say to him, "Prepare supper for me, and gird yourself and serve me, till I eat and drink; and afterward you shall eat and drink"? Does he thank the servant because he did what was commanded? So you also, when you have done all that is commanded you, say, "We are unworthy servants; we have only done what was our duty." '

If you are a slave, you must work like a slave. You may be tired after the long day in the field. It is after six o'clock. But there is no Christian Trade Union which regulates the hours of a man's service for Christ! (There are, of course, the Sunday Christians with a two-hour worshipping week.) If you are a slave, then you are never finished. Get my supper ready, says the master. You do not even deserve thanks, or praise, or testimonials, or honoraria. You are just a slave after all. What else should a slave do? Your own meal comes last in the priorities. And at the end, having done all, we recognize that we are unprofitable servants. We need more of this passion for service as Christians.

But, you say, surely a courteous master will thank the slave, even though it is only his duty? This is a parable, is it not, and Christ is not a harsh master, a slave-driver, surely? Right again, and this complementary truth is explained in Luke 12: 37: 'Blessed are those servants whom the master finds awake when he comes; truly, I say to you, he will gird himself and have them sit at table, and he will come and serve them.'

At first sight the two stories seem directly contradictory. But the aim of the two stories is different. The first story teaches us that we have no rights; the second, that we have a Master who is full of grace. He is no tyrant. We are slaves, but His service is not slavery. Though we are unworthy and unprofitable servants, yet He is merciful, generous, considerate, and always pouring blessings upon us down to the little details of daily life. The lesson of diligent, untiring service is there, but it is a labour of love for a beloved Master.

The diligence of the slave

We have already suggested that often, in opposing fanaticism, we are really shying away from diligence, and that, when we favour moderation, we are defending sloth. It is not only that we have done the things we ought not to have done, but that we have failed to do the things that we ought to have done. So often we are so concerned to live a life free of sin, that we are aiming merely at the absence of obvious and glaring inconsistency, a very negative type of holiness stressing what we refrain from doing; whereas the New Testament is urging upon us a positive holiness, and manifestation of positive virtues. It is not merely the absence of hate or grumbling that we seek, but the manifestation of love and cheerfulness. We must show diligence, then, and this word is used twice in the Authorized Version of 2 Peter 1: 5 and 10: 'And beside this, giving all *diligence*, add to your faith virtue; and to virtue knowledge; and to knowledge temperance;

and to temperance patience; and to patience godliness; and to godliness brotherly kindness; and to brotherly kindness charity . . . brethren, give *diligence* to make your calling and election sure.'

In thinking about diligence there seem to be three principles involved.

1. *To every one who has will more be given*

The story of the talents (Mt. 25: 14–30) tells us of the attitudes of the three servants to the talents committed to them and the attitude of their master to the results which they produce. The Lord commends those who are industrious and who use their opportunities diligently. It is all very undemocratic; one man has only one talent, while others have twice as much, or even five times as much! They do not have equality of ability, for it is 'to each according to his ability'; but they do have equality of opportunity, for all three have the same time in which to make the most of their several abilities. The one-talent man is punished for *sloth*. He is a 'wicked and slothful servant'. He is not diligent. The Lord does not sympathize with this poor fellow because he has only one talent after all. There is no excuse for sloth. It is wicked. He has not lost what he was given, but he has failed to multiply what he has.

All of us are prone to bury our opportunities. We usually feel that, later on, at some later date when we leave school, or when we graduate, or after we have married and settled down, or when we are promoted and have moved to a house of our own, or when the children are growing and we have a larger house, *then* at last we can do something. The future is always better than the present. We see our present opportunity as a single talent and fail to make use of it. Christ commends and rewards diligence: 'Well done, good and faithful servant.' The principle of verse 29, that 'to every one who has will more be given', is often repeated in the New Testament. The man who has opportunity but does not use it is termed 'worthless', and his talent is given to the one who has ten already and who has shown that he is willing to use them. The same principle is used in Mark 4: 25 about diligence in hearing the Word of God: the more you understand, the more you will be enabled to understand. It is a principle of spiritual compound interest. Be diligent and you will be blessed more and more. 'The path of the righteous is like the light of dawn, which shines brighter and brighter until full day' (Pr. 4: 18). The man who is diligent and righteous (opposites of slothful and wicked) experiences this increasing brightness and blessing.

2. *Every one to whom much is given, of him will much be required*

This principle makes it clear that more would be expected of the man with five talents. The man with one talent had produced nothing; had he doubled his capital he would doubtless have been commended. Had the five-talent man produced only one extra talent, he might deservingly have been rebuked. If the distribution of talents 'to each according to his ability' suggests that the allocation is not democratic, it is quite clear that none the less the judgment of results is fair and equable. Measurement of results is on a basis of diligence rather than ability.

We find this second principle in the story of the returning master (Lk. 12: 35–48). We are like those waiting for our master to return at any moment, and there is great blessing for those who are awake and ready. We all know that. But are we diligent and do we take to heart this fact that we know in our heads? It is one thing to have orthodox convictions about the Second Coming, and quite another actually to live in the light of that expectation. If things are not in order, what will the master do with this steward? The one who did not know will get only a light beating. But 'that servant who knew his master's will, but did not make ready or act according to his will, shall receive a severe beating'. This man knows what he ought to do, but he is not diligent. He knows it in his head, but fails to act with his hands.

Are we not in this position? Are there not things that we know that we ought to do that we are delaying action about? If there are some household repairs that our mothers or wives keep on reminding us about, or some mending that we have been given to do, we tend to delay, and all we suffer is a little domestic nagging. But what about the things which the Lord has asked us to do? We have this ideal before us of what a Christian ought to be like, but what are we doing about it? Much has been given to us; much will be required in the way of response. It is not enough to 'know' Christian doctrine; we must act upon it. These servant stories in the Gospels are very simple, but the message they bring is clear. If you are diligent you will find blessing. If you are blessed then you are responsible to be more diligent still. The Christian is somebody who is in action as a slave of Jesus Christ. He is never to be merely a stuffed specimen in a glass case; he is to be a working model. Being a Christian demands from us diligence in serving Christ.

3. *He who is faithful in a very little is faithful also in much*

In fact, the man with the one talent, had he been faithful in that little, would, like his two more diligent brethren, have been rewarded with opportunity to exhibit that same faithfulness in a larger sphere. So again we see the justice of God's principles of measuring success. Even though it was only one talent, he was expected to work with it.

This third principle about diligence is revealed in the amusing story of the unjust steward in Luke 16: 1-15.[2] The application here is that this man made an intelligent use of his present opportunities in order to secure his

[2] For a further exposition of this passage, see chapter 4 below.

future happiness (although, of course, his behaviour was dishonest, and he was a very unfaithful steward; but the parable is concerned with his forethought and common sense). It is an exhortation to use money with an eye to eternal results rather than merely temporal enjoyment. But the argument continues: if you have not been faithful in the unrighteous mammon, then who will entrust to you the true heavenly riches? If you are not faithful with other people's money, who will trust you with any of your own? At first the man is commended for his prudence and forethought, and then he is castigated for his unfaithfulness. The first argument is from the lesser to the greater, in the use that a man makes of earthly and heavenly currencies. But the second point is that a man's life is all of a piece, and that those who are scrupulous even in matters of minor importance are people who may be trusted also in larger matters. Diligence is not to be reserved for major issues, but to characterize the Christian in every aspect of his life, even in the smallest details.

Here, then, are three principles of diligence: more, much and little. Faithful in little, more is given, much is required sums up the progress in diligence. Let us give the last word on this to Solomon, who, for all his faults in other directions, cannot be accused of lack of diligence (see 1 Ki. 4), when he says: 'He who is slack in his work is a brother to him who destroys' (Pr. 18: 9).

The motivation of the slave

The Christian slave has his orders, but no taskmaster to stand over him with a whip. In one sense this is part of our problem with sloth. We are free to be lazy. Nobody stands over us to see that we are obeying. The slave of Christ is free and unsupervised. He is free to be diligent and he is free to be slothful. This is our problem, that if we are slothful we have only the querulous rebuke of a feeble conscience. Christian liberty is the opposite of legalism, not the opposite of slavery and service. It is *not* meant to be freedom to loaf or to be disobedient or independent of our Master. The Christian is in voluntary subjection as a slave. He is free—to serve.

In the Old Testament (Ex. 21: 1–7), where slavery had a fixed term of service and all slaves were released in the seventh year, there was a provision whereby a man might attach himself permanently to his master. He could say, if he wished, 'I love my master, my wife, and my children; I will not go out free.' Or, 'I want to be a slave of this man because he is good to me and I know that I can trust him. He gives me love and security and provides all my needs. I am happier as his slave than I ever could be out on my own.' Though Christ is our Master and Lord, He treats us not as slaves, but as friends and as brethren. Paul told Philemon that his one-time useless slave Onesimus was now coming back to him, as a brother beloved. The slave returned to be a slave, but the master was to welcome him as a brother. We have been purchased by the Lord Jesus, and we are His slaves; and yet He treats us as His brethren (*cf.* Rom. 8: 29; Heb. 2: 11, 12).

The motive, then, is not fear, but love. We serve Him, not out of duty, but out of desire to please Him. It is fitting that I should serve Him, for He is my Lord.

Suggestions for prayer and meditation

(It is more valuable to pray to the Lord about our problems than merely to recognize that they exist, and it would be better to spend time in prayer now than to go straight on to the next chapter.)

'What shall I render to the Lord for all his bounty to me? I will lift up the cup of salvation and call on the name of the Lord, I will pay my vows to the Lord in the presence of all his people' (Ps. 116: 12–14).

Have I ever made a clear, decisive acceptance of Christ as the Lord of my life? This may mean that I did not realize the implications of calling Him Lord at the time of conversion *or* that up till now I have never been more than a nominal Christian. But that matters little compared with the issue of whether I have made this decisive submission to obey Him in all things henceforth.

Am I calling Him 'Lord', and yet consciously disobeying or trying to forget something in which I do not want to obey Him? Am I prepared to put this right, *now*?

Do I have any experience of 'feet-washing', *i.e.* of humbling service of others? Are there ways in which I could be doing this, but have been holding back through pride —at home, at work or in the church?

Am I putting Christ first in everything, or only when there is no conflict with my personal ambition, prized material goals, those I must please if I am to succeed in life? Is my faith merely accessory or supplementary to my main purpose in life?

What opportunities do I have now that I can use for Christ? Am I using them to the full or letting them pass, hiding my talent in the ground? Are there ways in which my life can be useful to my Master, or am I a slothful and wicked servant?

Am I faithful in small things?

Do I really love my Master and therefore long to serve and please Him? Or is my service conditional on my own convenience?

> 'Give me the lowest place: not that I dare
>   Ask for that lowest place, but Thou hast died
> That I might live and share
>   Thy glory by Thy side.

Give me the lowest place: or if for me
   That lowest place too high, make one more low
Where I may sit and see
   My God and love Thee so.'

               CHRISTINA ROSETTI

3 LEISURE or URGENCY?

Take my moments and my days.

Time is an odd thing. Summer holidays, an afternoon with a fiancée, a stimulating conversation with an old friend—and time passes so very quickly. Other things pass too slowly—like waiting for that same fiancée to arrive, an hour's drill on the barrack square or ten minutes' drilling in the dentist's chair. If only time would go as slowly when we are interested as it does when we are bored. . . .

Age seems to make a difference. To a small child even a day seems a long time, and till next Christmas, or next birthday, an eternity. Then life starts to move in weeks as each weekend provides some respite from school, and then in months, and then in seasons, and then in years. The whole thing seems to gain acceleration with age. We read that, for the Lord, a thousand years is as one day, but that does not mean that He is indifferent to our use of time, for the same text (2 Pet. 3: 8) says that, to Him, one day is as a thousand years.

It has become customary for Christians to speak of the 'stewardship' of time and money. That is to say, we spend money and we use the same verb when we say that we 'spend' time. Time is a universal currency which may be used for buying things. It can be used directly to obtain money, *i.e.* we hire our services. Or it can be used for the pursuit of knowledge, the cultivation of friends, the enjoyment of pleasure, the gaining of experience—things which money cannot buy, but which can be purchased by expending time. The difference between one man and another often depends upon the skill with which he uses his time.

The Christian, who is, as we have seen, a grateful slave in the service of his Lord, wants to use his time in a way which will please the Master. His time is not his own, but belongs to the Lord Jesus. We are stewards of our time, to use it for Him.

Redeeming the time

The stewardship of time is, however, at first sight, not a subject about which the Bible appears to say very much directly. In the New Testament there seem to be only two references, or proof texts, found in the sister Epistles of Ephesians and Colossians (Eph. 5: 16; Col. 4: 5); but the contexts and sequence of thought in the two letters seem to be different, although expressed in identical words. This is the phrase rendered in AV as 'redeeming the time' and in RSV 'making the most of the time'. Even this, however, is not a straightforward exhortation to stewardship of time, for, as the commentators are eager to point out, the word used is not *chronos,* meaning duration of time in years, weeks, days and hours, but *kairos,* meaning a specific time or opportunity. It seems to mean a critical epoch, a special opportunity which may soon pass, and the injunction is to seize it and buy it up while it is still available. The Greek word *exagorazō,* translated 'redeem' (AV), really means to buy out of the market, so that following Simpson[1] we may best understand this to mean 'making a market of opportunities'. Anyone who has seen a woman at a bargain sale making a grab at something

[1] E. K. Simpson, *Epistle to the Ephesians (New London Commentary,* Marshall, Morgan and Scott, 1958), p. 124.

which is available now at a remarkably cheap price, seize it in triumph and go on looking for another 'good buy', may get something of the very vivid idea suggested by this phrase. We are to look out for opportunities, like bargains, and snatch them up whenever we can in the service of Christ and for the forwarding of His kingdom.

'Look carefully then how you walk, not as unwise men but as wise, making the most of the time, because the days are evil. Therefore do not be foolish, but understand what the will of the Lord is. And do not get drunk with wine, for that is debauchery; but be filled with the Spirit, addressing one another in psalms and hymns and spiritual songs, singing and making melody to the Lord with all your heart, always and for everything giving thanks in the name of our Lord Jesus Christ to God the Father' (Eph. 5: 15–20). This context seems concerned, first, with behaviour, how you walk (*i.e.* live), and suggests that, when we have spare time, we use it not for debauchery but for what some people call 'devotional exercises', and if that sounds too much like muscular Christianity, let us call it worship, praise and prayer. In the first century, when many Christians were literally slaves, there was little time for leisure outside working hours, and here is direction on how to spend it. Do not fritter the time away in the wineshops, but seek out other Christians and take the rare opportunity for fellowship while you have it. At the same time he indicates 'always and for everything' (verse 20) that all our time is to be marked by a sense of thankfulness to God, and then he goes on to give practical directions about family life and relationships, and then attitudes towards one's work and one's employers (5: 21–6: 9).

In Colossians, after dealing with family relationships and labour relations, Paul asks prayer for his own proclamation of the gospel and continues: 'that I may make it clear, as I ought to speak. Conduct yourselves wisely toward outsiders, making the most of the time. Let your speech always be gracious, seasoned with salt, so that you may know how you ought to answer every one' (Col. 4: 4–6). Here, then, the context seems to be that of evangelism, one's attitude to non-Christians and thus to taking opportunities for witness and soul-winning.

However, as is often the case, this matter is not one which may be studied merely by looking up the word 'time' in a concordance. It is more commonly dealt with in terms of the necessity for diligence and injunctions against idleness and sloth.

Talents and pounds

In the parables of the talents and the pounds (Mt. 25: 14–30; Lk. 19: 12–26), there is a man who has a certain amount of capital and 'a long time' (Mt. 25: 19), but who does nothing with it. It is not the possession of the talent, so much as the time to use it to gain interest, which prompts the rebuke, 'You wicked and slothful servant!' Whatever we take the talents and pounds to represent— natural gifts, salvation, or whatever it is—the men are expected to do something with what they have, even if they have less than others. And they are given *time* in order to do this. If the master had returned the very next day, then no-one would have had time to gain anything, and none would be worthy of congratulation or condemnation. It is thus the use of time which becomes significant in both these parables. Whatever the differences, this feature is common to both, that they may be understood as dealing with the stewardship of time. The aim of the parables would seem to be to remind us also that one day we too shall have to give an account of our stewardship, of how we have used our time and opportunities, whether we have been industrious servants of our Master, or whether we have been casual and indisciplined.

The uncertainty of life

One common emphasis which is made to encourage Christians to use their time to the full is the uncertainty of life. That is, not only may there be a variation of ability or number of talents, but also there may be a variation in the length of the opportunity. The NEB translation of 'redeeming the time' is: 'Use the present opportunity to the full.' Some men, like David Brainerd, Henry Martyn or Borden of Yale, were to die very early, but they used their time *to the full*.

'Come now, you who say, "Today or tomorrow we will go into such and such a town and spend a year there and trade and get gain"; whereas you do not know about tomorrow. What is your life? For you are a mist that appears for a little time and then vanishes. Instead you ought to say, "If the Lord wills, we shall live and we shall do this or that." As it is, you boast in your arrogance. All such boasting is evil. Whoever knows what is right to do and fails to do it, for him it is sin' (Jas. 4: 13–17). Not only are we reminded that our plans for tomorrow are always subject to the divine permission, but our life is like a mist, a puff of smoke, and tomorrow we may be dead. And then there is the application, that if we know what is right to do and we do not do it, this is sin. The implication is that we should not put off until tomorrow the righteous thing we should do today.

The return of the Master

A second kindred emphasis, found repeatedly in the New Testament, is the return of the Master. It may not be death which catches us unawares, but it may be the Lord's return which tests the validity of what we are doing. Is my form of employment one which is pleasing to the Lord? Or my form of recreation, for that matter?

'Who then is the faithful and wise servant, whom his master has set over his household, to give them their food at the proper time? Blessed is that servant whom his master when he comes will find so doing. Truly, I say to you, he will set him over all his possessions. But if that wicked servant says to himself, "My master is delayed," and begins to beat his fellow servants, and eats and drinks with the drunken, the master of that servant will come on a day when he does not expect him and at an hour he does not know, and will punish him, and put him with the hypocrites; there men will weep and gnash their teeth' (Mt. 24: 45–51). The man here is a steward who has a responsibility towards other people, and has been given provisions by his master expressly for their benefit. If the man misuses his authority, and the opportunity for service to others, and appropriates to himself what was really meant for them, then the Master will come unexpectedly and punish him.

As we do not know when our Lord will be coming, we shall always be eager to be found doing that which will please Him. Clearly the idea of being 'caught' like a naughty little boy, whose mother comes home to find him snacking in the pantry, is only part of the truth. The Christian will remember that all that he does is in the sight of God; it is not a question of being surprised by a hitherto uncomprehending master. Both the passages concerning work in Ephesians and Colossians make this point, that we have an all-knowing Master in the heavens who is not deceived. We can do things when the boss is looking and slack when he is away; but God is not mocked like that.

The danger of being a sluggard

The chief difference between a snail and a slug is that you can see when the latter is doing nothing. In the book of Proverbs it is the woman in the house who is the model of diligence. She, the 'good wife' of chapter 31, does her husband good 'all the days of her life'; she rises 'while it is yet night' and 'her lamp does not go out at night'. She 'does not eat the bread of idleness' and we see how industriously she occupies herself, to the advancement of her husband (verse 23), the blessing of the poor and needy (verse 20), and the general health and prosperity of her family, who one and all rise up and call her blessed. Her secret is that she 'fears the Lord' (verse 30) and she makes really good use of her time. There is no corresponding section on the ideal husband!

Earlier in Proverbs, however, we are treated to several terse descriptions of the weakness of the sluggard, who by contrast is usually described in the masculine gender. We note his characteristics:

1. *He cannot plan ahead.* He 'does not plough in the autumn; he will seek at harvest and have nothing' (20: 4). The ant is hard at work in the summer (6: 6 ff.) collecting food for the hard days ahead, while lazybones sleeps the days away. He is just too drowsy to get on with what he knows needs to be done. There is a lack of forethought and common sense in preparing for the future. It is the unprepared servant all over again. Today we meet this most commonly in such comments as 'I hadn't realized that the days passed so quickly' and 'I don't know where time goes to these days.'

2. *He cannot get down to work.* 'The soul of the sluggard craves, and gets nothing, while the soul of the diligent is richly supplied' (13: 4). The sluggard recognizes that he has a need. He knows that for the good of his soul he needs to study the Bible, to pray for God's blessing; but while he wants to do this, being a sluggard he fails to act. The diligent man is more conscientious and acts and so is richly supplied.

3. *He is more concerned with problems than overcoming them.* 'The way of a sluggard is overgrown with thorns,

but the path of the upright is a level highway' (15: 19). He is so beset with difficulties, poor fellow, that he can only sit down and mope about it, like his friend (26: 13) who will not go out of doors for fear there may be a lion out there. Such people make difficulties for themselves. It excuses inaction. The Christian man meets difficulties but is concerned to overcome them; indeed these are the stuff of growth and maturity. The fun is to beat the problems. But the sluggard, who is here contrasted with the upright (that is, the sinfulness of sloth is recognized), has many problems of his own making. Because of his lack of integrity, he is a lazy man.

4. *He is a hindrance to others and a destructive influence.* 'He who is slack in his work is a brother to him who destroys' (18: 9). We know today that it is shoddy workmanship in cars, aeroplanes, buildings and the like which is the cause of fatal accidents. This is also true in some offices and leadership in the church, where negligence of responsibility may lead to a breakdown of fellowship. A church may be disintegrated through foolish negligence and laziness as well as by Satanic attack.

Leaders of Youth Groups or Christian Unions have a real responsibility here. Do they just keep the wheels moving and run the same old programme on an *ad hoc* basis—we must get a speaker for next week; what shall we ask him to talk about?—and doing a minimum of work? Or is there a real assessment of present weaknesses and a programme planned to meet the actual needs of the present situation? Some leaders just enjoy their prestige, sitting on the band-wagon, which has been set rolling through the hard work of their predecessors, instead of setting a clear course, making strenuous efforts to add increasing momentum, and attaining specific goals. A good deal of leadership degenerates into mere organizing, and a minimum even of that.

The sluggard is a man who does not steward his time for the glory of God. It may not even occur to him that

TAKE MY LIFE

time is a precious commodity to be used in this way. Let us be up and doing, while we have time before the darkness and the winter come.

A time for . . . .

From Proverbs one goes on naturally to Ecclesiastes, with its earthy common sense, its reminder to the young to serve God while they may (12: 1), and its poetically beautiful but tragic description of old age (thank God we do not have to live eternally in these aging bodies, but may look forward to getting new ones after experiencing the biological necessity of death), and the pessimism that must obtain where there is no revelation of the life to come. But we take his reminder that there is a time for everything (3: 1ff.) as an Old Testament version of redeeming the time, of making a market of opportunities, of using all times appropriately to the glory of God. There are occasions appropriate to the young, and only to them, and there are occasions for the old (especially in the Orient) which others are too young and inexperienced to use. The young are not meant to spend their time hankering to be older, nor the older mourning the good old days and wishing they could be young again. There is a need for some good Christian existentialism at both points, a realization of that which is appropriate to the present. How many of us have wasted years, frittered away time, when it was not appropriate? How many, for example, have played at courting when marriage was not even possible for years to come? How many have grown bitter, longing for leadership, when at their present age 'followership' was more appropriate, until they had more experience?

Years at the university as a student are manifestly 'a time to study', and not primarily for recreation and dilly-dallying. There is a deal of difference between balanced

54

recreation and an abandoned worship of the sporting gods of field and river, just as there is a difference between directed widening of interests and hours spent in profit-less superficialities over endless cups of expensive coffee.[2]

Time and motion studies

We are all familiar with the efficiency expert approach—'creatures all of time and "pace"'—bent on discovering the minimum effort required to produce the best results. All unnecessary movements are cut out; the essential tools must be in the most convenient spot, the raw materials on the other side, and so forth. This approach to one's time can be interesting—or soul-destroying! Not a minute must be wasted. Between this time and this we read our Bibles; after lunch, for twenty-two and a half minutes we read a biography, and so forth. We look for the wasted moments, like the mustard left on the plate, and determine some method of using them profitably. There is a value in this kind of approach, especially for those of casual temperament; but there are limits. Men are meant to live like men and not like robots. We all appreciate that busy men have little time to spare, but none the less we do not like to be ushered in and hustled out to fit the schedule. Too much of a set schedule can become an idol, if we get irritated when something comes along to interfere with it. There is a joy in meeting the calm, un-hurried people, who in spite of all they get through have time for all of us. Some people can organize their time —they have that temperament; and it is certainly better to be organized than to be in a perpetual dither of rush and disorganization. At the same time it is better to be serene than in a perpetual hustle.

Most of us could be better organized than we are; and

2 See O. R. Barclay, *The Christian's Approach to University Life* (IVF, 1963), especially pp. 14ff.

perhaps even more than organization, what is needed is a settling of priorities. For example, we must decide which periodicals and papers really are worth reading, and which are not. We may fritter away hours on trivia in newspapers, pointless television-viewing, and so on. When we relax, let us relax. But there seems to be an awful lot which is neither one thing nor the other. It is easy to get into the state where one rarely reads a solid book, and one presumes that the worst offenders will not even be reading a slight paperback like this!

The cost of living

One day, in order to save money, I was about to take a somewhat indirect and roundabout journey rather than take a taxicab. A fellow missionary, who belonged to a mission well known for their sacrificially low level of subsistence, asked if my time was really worth as little as that! Work out what your time is worth per hour of working day, he said. As soon as I did this, I realized, as he had already done, that to spend all that *time* in travel, when it could be done so much faster, was in fact not saving money at all but wasting it! At the very lowest level our time is worth whatever it takes to support us; at the highest it is worth whatever we allow the Holy Spirit to use us to do. The Christian is not concerned to be mercenary, but to him time is precious because it is a gift from God. *He* gives me my days.

Time may be a very valuable commodity. Take the average committee. There is the old joke about keeping minutes and wasting hours, but a committee really does cost time and thus money. It costs the total of the value of the labour of those taking part, plus the travel costs of those who attend it. Usually these all appear as a hidden subsidy, because people pay their own fares and give their own time. But this means that late arrival costs a lot of time, and so does quibbling over minor points, or not listening and having to be told again. It costs money as well as time. When this committee becomes an international one, and people are travelling considerable distances to attend, when even five minutes represent a great sum of money laid out, woe betide the man who does not stick to the point or who introduces quite unnecessary problems that could be dealt with at some other time. Student committees often suffer from inexperienced chairmanship and grasshopper-minded members, and talk round in ever-widening circles, ending up without having decided anything. Gossiping for hours about irrelevancies far into the night is very relaxing, but that is not what a committee is for!

If time has such a value, then we need to be scrupulously careful during our working hours to give to our employer value for time. Our attention needs to be given fully to what we are doing if we are to give full value for our time. We would not dream of stealing money from an employer; yet to work half-heartedly, even for a day, may be the equivalent of this, for we are being paid for what we are not doing!

Most students these days are on grants provided out of public money. The taxpayer, returning tired and grimy from his day of toil, and forced to listen to the overloud frothings of students returning on a university town bus, may with some justification glower askance at the apparently idle students with leisure for sports and social activities indulged in at his expense. In our use of student time we have a clear moral obligation to society.

Instant methods

Today quick, easy methods are the vogue. The days of Mrs Beeton's leisurely methods have given way to the 'instant whip' and the 'cake mix'. Instalment plans make it possible for people to use and enjoy things before they have paid for them. Every effort is made to 'save time' and the washing-machine advertisements are eager to point out that their particular machine liberates the housewife hours earlier than her forbears might have expected on a washday. Does our desire to be good stewards of our time mean that we shall rush for the 'instant' approach? There is certainly no point in spending longer on the household chores than one needs, but it is worth reflecting that there are no short cuts to success in fields such as education, friendship, marriage, parenthood or, for that matter, in Christian sanctification.

In spite of the passion for the condensed book, the digested article, and even the reduction of Shakespeare to serial strip form, a real education still takes time. There seems to be less scholarship today than there used to be. John Stuart Mill was a genius, but it is staggering to see what he had mastered by the age of thirteen. Adolf Harnack once convened a seminar on the Pastoral Epistles in which it was a condition of participation to memorize the Epistles in Greek, German and English, and to be prepared to discuss in German, French or English. Some of us have perhaps tried to read some of those infuriating Bible commentaries where choice comments are given in the original, whether it be Greek, Latin, French or German, and it puts most of us moderns at considerable disadvantage. A real education takes time, and it is a tragedy, when we are so limited by our fields of specialization, that we are so very ignorant of other fields of knowledge. Even in countries where there is a theory of more general education, ignorance seems just as abysmal, only more general!

The Christian, of course, is not called upon to be a kind of walking *Pears Encyclopedia,* but a knowledge of history, philosophy, economics, literature and so on can be used in the service of Christian apologetics, quite apart from its intrinsic value. This does not mean that we should belong to innumerable dilettante groups, the more so if this is made an excuse for worldly indulgences and inactivity in specifically Christian spheres of service. Because we are men with a Master and a purpose in life, there will have to be a cutting away of things which are perfectly good in themselves, but for which we just do not have time.

Human relationships

One cannot organize one's relationships by the clock. Charles Hummel relates [3] how, after hours and months spent working together and doing things together, a Chinese classmate said solemnly one evening, 'Charlie, I consider you my friend.' The word 'friend' is so often debased, but to this Chinese student it was reserved for someone whom he had come to know and love and trust. In these busy days friendship can become a debased word referring only to chance acquaintances who happen to be thrown together for a while. At the end of each year Japanese will send cards to thank people for kindnesses done to them years before; they never forget a kindness and are meticulous in expressing gratitude. Friendship is a sphere in which Christians should excel, but so often we are superficial, and there is a lack of understanding and love, and for this reason we can be ineffective in introducing others to the Lord Jesus. Non-Christians may sometimes be better at it. Camus has a charming description[4] of a night swim, when Rieux, the doctor who survived, and Tarrou his friend, who later perished in the plague-smitten city, take a break from fighting the epidemic. 'Turning to Tarrou, he caught a glimpse on his friend's face of the same happiness, a happiness that forgot nothing . . . neither had said a word, but they were

[3] Article on 'Short Cuts' in *Sunday School Times*, 13 June 1964.
[4] Albert Camus, *The Plague* (Methuen, 1962), p. 210.

conscious of being perfectly at one, and that the memory of this night would be cherished by them both.'

Sometimes we just fail to get through to the other person: we may be interested in somebody as a soul instead of as a man. Real friendship can be costly, the more so when it may seem sometimes to be one-sided, until mutual confidence is established. We may overlook the deeply sensitive attitudes of an overseas student, for example, fearful of patronage or curiosity of alien novelty, and yet longing for genuine friendship. So often, Christian though we claim to be, we can still be selfish and concerned primarily with our own advantage in every relationship, without true perceptivity of the sensitivities of other people. God grant that we might be the kind of person who is honestly interested in and concerned for others, with a Christ-like warmth of personality, and an eye-twinkling integrity, which establishes bridgeheads with others. God give me involvement with others for their blessing and His glory.

The same need for spending time together is obviously true of marriage. What kind of monster would it be that regulated courtship with his eye on his watch? Yet so often, when the honeymoon is over, it is the wife who feels neglected in the allocation of the husband's time. There may still be time to talk, but not enough to communicate in terms of the real problems and longings of the heart. The same goes for the children, for modern life so often seems to demand the earlier departure and the later return from work, so that the father may not see much of smaller children for days on end. An added problem for Christians is that, whereas the 'secular man' may take his children off for a day in the car on the Sunday, the active Christian may be so busy in a round of services and Sundays schools that his children feel neglected. This may work the other way round as the children become older and neglect their parents. *Cheaper by the Dozen* is a hilarious tale of how an efficiency expert sought to regulate his large family by similar principles at home, and amid all the organization the beauty of the family relationship was preserved.[5] None the less, family relationships cannot normally be regulated by the clock, but demand our joyous and prodigal use of time.

There seems a danger, in talking of the stewardship of time, that we neglect these important areas of life, and grudge time spent on those who have the biggest claim on our time. How was it that the Lord Jesus came to have that child on His knee when He was in 'the house' at Capernaum (Mk. 9: 33–37)? If it was the house of Peter (*cf*. Mk. 1: 21, 29), then it suggests that the Lord had made time to play with Peter's children and to win their trust (Mk. 9: 42).

Spiritual fellowship

We all face the steady pressure of increasing responsibility. However busy the student may feel himself to be, when he graduates he will immediately feel pressed for time. Maintaining a regular 'Quiet Time' unhurriedly in the Lord's presence, reading the Bible, hearing His word and responding in prayer from the heart, becomes harder. Then courtship and marriage become an important claim on our time, not to be denied, and time becomes a scarcer commodity than ever. When the Lord blesses us with children as well, they seem to require urgent attention in the early morning hours, and even if they require nothing they seem to delight to provide noisy interruption before breakfast. The struggle to keep a Quiet Time and to have time, not to mention quiet, seems to get harder rather than easier as the years go by. Yet how important it is to 'make time for the Lord'. No friendship can thrive on cursory 'good morning' and 'good evening' nods, and a

[5] F. B. Gilbreth and E. M. G. Carey, *Cheaper by the Dozen* (Heinemann, 1948).

Christmas card once a year. Even a busy Christian worker may become stale and estranged from his Lord, and need renewal in His presence. This requires stewardship and discipline of time.

A bachelor friend of mine, who would be free of some of these distractions, used to declare that if a young person had not got down to solid Bible study and mastered the basic doctrines by the age of twenty-five, he never would do so! It is certainly true that 'the earlier the better', while we have the habit of study and our memories are still plastic and retentive. But there are no short cuts to knowledge or growth. Reading a book on 'Ten Steps to Christian Maturity' or 'Sanctification Made Simple' may help to give some ideas on what we should be doing and how we should be praying, but none the less the taking of these steps is still going to take us a lifetime.

Use of Sunday

Good George Herbert writes:

> 'The Sundaies of man's life,
>   Threaded together on time's string,
> Make bracelets to adorn the wife
>   Of the eternal glorious King.'

There is perhaps nothing more characteristically Christian than the keeping of Sunday, the setting aside of the first day of the week for a specific remembrance of God's grace and meeting together with other Christians to rejoice together in Him. While recognizing that every day is to be hallowed to the Lord, there is yet a place for making one day a particular day for His special service. It is a day when we can, as it were, symbolize our priorities both to ourselves and to others. It is the Christian's weekly festival when he joyously commemorates that first

Easter day, and for many it is a weekly remembrance of the day when they were converted and first met Christ. The Christian is not bound by any sabbath law, for Christ has decreed that this day is not to be kept for itself, but for the benefit of mankind. At the same time, He is the Lord of the sabbath, and it is a day when we can give Him pre-eminence. This should not mean that the day becomes a mad chase from one service or meeting to another, from dawn till well after dusk, so that Monday is needed to recuperate from Sunday. As Sunday is often the one day in the week when the whole family are at home together, it does give a good opportunity to make each Sunday a memorably different day. There seems to be a need that we should also be good stewards of our Sundays and make them special in a Christian way.

Disproportionate use of time

The new Japanese version of Philippians 1: 10 gives Paul's second prayer request for his Philippian converts as, 'that you may discern what is important.' This is of course the crucial issue in our use of time. To decide between what is an obviously right course of action and an obviously wrong one, or even a slightly doubtful one, is really not so very difficult. The difficulty arises because we just do not have time to do everything that we should like to do, and so we have to choose between two good alternatives. We have to make choices, and by making choices we grow in Christian maturity.

Christians, as we have seen, have certain priorities to maintain. Like everybody else, we have family relationships, professional responsibilities, work to do and obligations to fulfil. We do not regard these as of only secondary importance: precisely because we are Christians, and it is intrinsic to our whole attitude of life, we know how desperately important it is to try to excel in the humdrum things of daily living. But it is far from easy to decide how to balance all the various demands upon our limited time, so that it becomes a harmonious whole, a living, dramatized psalm of praise to the glory of our God.

It is so easy to use time disproportionately, to spend a whole morning on some fiddling little item that is not worth more than five minutes, to spend hours polishing an essay, not because it would really improve its intrinsic worth or the value of the ideas contained in it, but out of a kind of distorted vanity. We can spend far too much time on some things, and far too little on others. Too much time, perhaps, on the details of organizing some Christian meeting, or designing posters for it, and too little time on befriending the people who come to it. People are more important than things, and relationships than decorations. We need to pray for ourselves and for each other, as Paul did, that we may 'discern what is important'. The difference between the disorganized person on the edge of a breakdown and the calm, unflappable type is often that the second has determined what is important and does not waste time, anxiety or energy on the non-essentials.

Examples

The apostle Paul, in addition to a full preaching ministry with house-to-house visiting (Acts 20: 20), was also working for his own support, and that of others, so that he could remind the Ephesian elders that 'these hands ministered to my necessities, and to those who were with me' (verse 34). We also know that it was in the same city that Paul took the lecture-hall of Tyrannus for daily meetings. The Western text (Acts 19: 9) adds 'between eleven and four', that is, during the siesta time when many had little thought apart from sleep in the middle of the day. After a busy morning's work on tent-making, when Tyrannus

had already finished for the day, Paul is there preaching
to all who will come and hear.

Think of the prodigious labours of Richard Baxter,
who seems to have been a walking museum of patho-
logical conditions and always sickly, renowned for his
house-to-house ministry in Kidderminster, going from
family to family catechizing them, yet whose published
works in the Orme edition occupy twenty-three volumes.
This represents only a part of his total output, for he
wrote 'about one hundred and twenty eight books'
according to his own recollection, and all told what we
have of his writing would take sixty octavo volumes with
a total of thirty-five thousand closely printed pages! It
is this man who wrote: 'I have these forty years been
sensible of the sin of losing time; I could not spare an
hour.' One of the first demands on his time were his
studies and he pursued this aim with a single-minded love
for learning which the crowded years could never abate.
'The whole man and the whole time is all too little in so
great a work.'[6] One gets some idea of how this man
occupied himself in the following words: 'And concerning all my writings I must confess that my own judgement
is that fewer well studied and polished had been better
. . . for the Saints Rest I had four months vacancy to
write it (but in the midst of continual languishing and
medicine). But for the rest, I wrote them in the crowd of
all my other imployments which would allow me no great
leisure for polishing and exactness, or any ornament.'[7]

But to be a little more up to date, I can remember some
words of a certain professor of law which made a very
deep impression on me as a student. He was very active
in Christian work, and had just been awarded a coveted
higher degree. This had involved the submission of books
and articles totalling hundreds of thousands of words, and

[6] Marcus Loane, *Makers of Religious Freedom* (IVF, 1960), p. 165.
[7] *Autobiography* (Everyman edition), p. 103.

when I asked how he had found time, he replied simply, with a smile: 'I work.' [8]

But these were exceptional men! But were they busy because they were exceptional, or were they exceptional because they were busy? And were they not busy because they were Christians and because there is much to be done for the glory of God? For them time is a precious thing to be used to the utmost for God and for His kingdom.

The young American Roman Catholic Doctor Dooley, working in a hospital up-country in Laos, with the threat of an early death from cancer hanging over him, quoted Robert Frost:

'The woods are lovely, dark and deep,
But I have promises to keep
And miles to go before I sleep'

and then added, 'I believe the important thing is not how long we live, but what we do in the days allotted to us.'

What are *we* doing?

Suggestions for prayer and meditation

What is my attitude to my use of time: is it my aim to use it for my Lord? Should I not make a habit of reviewing my use of time in prayer at the beginning and end of the day?

Am I using my opportunities for Christ, or do I not really give the matter a thought?

Am I in danger of being a 'sluggard' and haphazard over time?

[8] Some people 'do' too much, sometimes even engaging in Christian work to the neglect of their families, the detriment of their work and their own souls, and the despair of their friends. Some need a word on not neglecting their wives and children, or their own personal relationship with Christ. See my *Consistent Christianity* (IVF, 1960), p. 42.

Are the years just going by without achieving anything?

What are my goals in my use of my time as a Christian?

Am I neglecting my own family or my own children?

Have I been neglecting to have a Quiet Time?

Do I potter and dither about?

Am I always in a mad rush?

Dear Lord, grant to me both diligence and serenity in my use of time, and help me to know what is important, that in the days which You give to me I may glorify You.

'Are there not twelve hours in the day? . . . Night comes, when no one can work' (Jn. 11: 9; 9: 4).

> 'Only twelve short hours—O never
>   Let the sense of urgency
> Die in us, Good Shepherd, ever
>   Let us search the hills with Thee.'

AMY CARMICHAEL

4

THRIFT
or GENEROSITY?

Take my silver and my gold;
Not a mite would I withhold.

'Nothing offers so practical a test of our love for Christ
or for others as does our attitude to money and possessions. Nor does anything so test our claim to be delivered
from this present evil world. The attitude of the un-
converted man to money is too widespread to be other
than well-known. The world asks how much we own;
Christ asks how we use it. The world thinks more of
getting; Christ thinks more of giving. The world asks
what we give, Christ asks how we give; the former thinks
of the amount, the latter of the motive. Men ask how
much we give; the Bible how much we keep. To the un-
converted, money is a means of gratification: to the converted, a means of grace; to the one an opportunity of
comfort, to the other an opportunity of consecration.'
These characteristically forthright words of Bradford
chemist and Christian leader Fred Mitchell, in his
thorough and excellent booklet *The Stewardship of
Money*,[1] are a fitting introduction to this chapter. The
present writer acknowledges his debt to that book and
to those whose generous and loving example of giving
has been the practical illustration of these same principles.

To whom does your money belong? How much did you
bring with you when you were born and how much will

[1] *The Stewardship of Money* (IVF, 1951), p. 7.

you take out with you when you die? The books for the period between are bound to balance, but on what has it all been expended? One thing is certain, that if we meet with Christ our attitude to money and possessions is bound to change, or at least to be challenged. Chapters 16–21 of Luke's Gospel might almost be a 'Christian Treatise on the Use of Money', so much do they contain of practical teaching about the use of money, in direct precept, in thought-stimulating parable and in living example. We meet the rich man who was clothed in purple and fine linen and feasted sumptuously every day, and who rather conveniently ignored the beggar sitting at his gate. We meet the rich young ruler who was commanded to sell all that he had and to distribute to the poor, to have treasure in heaven and to follow the Lord Jesus; but he refused the challenge. Then we pass one of those poor men, another beggar, this time a blind one, sitting by the roadside at Jericho, and Jesus heals him by opening his eyes. Then we meet another rich man, who comes scrambling down from the tree, to welcome Jesus to his home. This chief tax collector gives half of his goods to feed the poor and returns fourfold what he has defrauded. No doubt the formerly blind beggar was one of the poor who benefited that day, so that Jesus made the poor man richer and the rich man poorer; but in doing so He made both of them happier. What the rich man Dives failed to see he could do for the beggar at his gate, and what the rich young ruler refused to do when it was brought to his attention, Zacchaeus the publican volunteered to do on that joyous and never-to-be-forgotten day when Jesus invited Himself to stay at Zacchaeus' house and brought him tumbling down that tree-trunk in his haste to receive Him joyfully. It is all in the context when you read your Bible several chapters at a time and not just verses at a time. Let us look at the whole passage more closely.

What money is for

Luke 16: 1–9 contains the entertaining story of the un-scrupulous steward, who, learning that he was about to be sacked, used his opportunities while he had them to ensure that he would be provided for afterwards. Dorothy Sayers[2] portrays the ex-tax collector Matthew, with his cockney accent, as one who knows all about sharp finan-cial practice and 'cooking the books', enjoying a regen-erate chuckle over such unregenerate lack of scruple. The Lord commends the man for his prudence and foresight; that is, he used the money that he had control of in the present to ensure his security in the future. He was a son of this world and utterly dishonest, breaking both the eighth and ninth commandments quite blatantly. But though he was a rogue, he is commended for being wise and shrewd. For money is to be used here and now to make friends who will greet us afterwards in heaven; that is, we are to use 'the mammon of unrighteousness' (*i.e.* money) for the sake of the work of God and the extension of His kingdom.

Putting it in mercenary terms, we are to ensure that when we get to heaven there will be friends there to greet us! When some enter the portals of heaven with a shout there will be a joyful throng to meet us—strangers, many of them, former lepers, tribesmen, children, men from every nation under heaven—people are there in heaven because we used our money wisely. Our gift of money then made possible this welcome meeting now. How very unspiritual! But this is surely the meaning of verse 9. Here is a way in which earthly money may be transferred to the bank of heaven, by giving it away wisely and thoughtfully to those in need. There are no pockets in shrouds, but there is a way to send money on ahead—

[2] D. L. Sayers, *Man born to be King* (Gollancz, 1941), pp. 113, 118.

give it away! Not just anyhow of course, but shrewdly and wisely[3] as the unjust steward did. It was said of Henry Martyn's friend and biographer, John Sargent, that he seemed 'scarcely able to comprehend the pleasure of owning anything, unless he could give it to another'.

Christ goes on to give further instruction about money, about faithfulness in small matters being an indication of suitability for greater trust (making it quite clear, incidentally, that the steward was not commended for his dishonesty). Christ then makes the further point that if we cannot be trusted in money matters, who can entrust to us the true heavenly riches? The Evangelist notes that the Pharisees who heard this were 'lovers of money' (verse 14) and Christ delivers a stern rebuke as they scoff at His teaching and says that what is exalted among men, that is, the commonly-held worldly admiration of wealth and riches, is an abomination in the sight of God. We need to drive this home to ourselves, that the attitudes to money by which we have been influenced since childhood, and the amassing of status symbols, which is the commonly-accepted measure of success among us, may be abomination before God.

Modern advertising plays on this, suggesting that nobody who is anybody can afford to be without whatever it is they have to sell, and the sense of competition with one's neighbours is certainly 'exalted among men' (and women!) today. The prosperous West, with its false sense of superiority towards those in less materially developed countries, sometimes laughs at the tendency of simpler peoples to get a craze for some new thing, be it shoes,

---

[3] The idea of using money generously and wisely is not to be taken as suggesting that the church's main problem is that of fund-raising. Indeed there seem to be dangers in certain parts of the world that churches may degenerate into fund-raising organizations for the sustaining of good causes, notably their own survival. If a church is short of money in a prosperous society, it is usually symptomatic of a deeper spiritual malady.

spectacles or scooters, and blindly fails to notice that a great deal of visiting other people's homes and comparing boilers and heating systems, furniture and contemporary decoration is only a very slightly sophisticated form of the same kind of slavish imitation.

Such slavish conformity is, oddly enough, not confined to older people, and even those most determined not to be 'square' seem equally enslaved by current fashions, even those alleged to indicate revolt against convention and conformity. Students are nauseated by a hypocritical and stereotyped society, and see clearly the superficialities of the society against which they are in revolt, only to become equally bound to follow the craze of the moment. 'Keeping up with the Joneses' has its parallels in every age-group of society.

The full pocket and the blind eye

This principle of using money to ensure that we are welcomed into the heavenly habitations is then illustrated (negatively) by the story of Dives and Lazarus (Lk. 16: 19–31). This is not, of course, a kind of political parable to show that all wicked capitalists go to hell and the downtrodden proletariat go to heaven, for faith (Abraham is the father of all who believe, Gal. 3: 7; Rom. 4: 16) and repentance (verse 30), or lack of it, are both implied. The point of the parable is not the financial comparison, but the utter finality of death in fixing the eternal consequences of our attitudes in life. All the same, it is clear that the rich man's sin which is stressed here is his extravagance and self-indulgence, coupled with his indifference to the needs of those around him. He had a full pocket, which he used for his own enjoyment, and a blind eye, so that he failed to see others whom he might have helped with his money.

Most of us are content to keep quiet about an economic system which keeps our own standard of living going up, while we know that in other parts of the world (and in some less fortunate parts of our own) many people are living on a bare subsistence level. 'Bless all natives in foreign parts—and keep them there' expresses this attitude.[4] It may be in some measure true to suggest that people who have never known anything better could not miss what we have learnt to think of as essential, but does not this parable challenge us here? Certainly we recognize that men are not equal in intellectual ability and money-making capacity, but such inequality arises more from the accident of birth, nationality and opportunity than from other causes. To some these may seem to be social rather than religious issues, but Dives does not seem to have been able to convince Abraham of this, and in the enlightenment of an eternal perspective (when he got to the place from which he could get a better view) he seems to have recognized his own sin and to have wanted to see his brothers (presumably now enjoying his capital; it seems very unlikely that he left it to the poor!) delivered from the same judgment.

Money is hard to part from

Luke 18: 18–25. The rich young ruler has a concern for spiritual values; he desires to inherit eternal life. He insists that he has been scrupulous in obeying the commandments of God. The Lord, we read (Mk. 10: 21), loved the man and invited him to follow Him, to become a disciple, adding the condition that he first give away all that he had to the poor, and so have treasure in heaven. Here, then, is a man with a spiritual motive, a holy life, an invitation from Christ Himself, and yet in the final issue he values his material possessions more than spiritual treasure, and he goes away sorrowful. We are not to

[4] David Head, *He sent Leanness* (Epworth, 1959), p. 43.

judge from this that Christ commanded all to give away their riches. We know that for a time He and His disciples were supported through the generosity of a number of people, including Joanna and Susanna 'who provided for them out of their means' (Lk. 8: 3). It seems, therefore, that these people were not faced with this same challenge. Presumably for him riches had become an idol from which he had to be parted. This is a warning to the rich that a respectable life is not enough if possessions have become an idol which prevents us from following Jesus whole-heartedly.

This passage is followed by the famous words that it is easier to thread a great hawser or cable (Gk. *kamilos* is very similar to *kamēlos,* meaning a camel) through the eye of a needle than for a rich man to get into heaven. The rich young ruler had his opportunity. Dives too had had a poor beggar at his gate who would have threaded the fat overloaded cable of his life through the needle's eye of salvation, had he been given the opportunity. But the young man refused a specific invitation to follow. His attention was drawn to what he had to do, but he refused to do it. It is not surprising, then, that among the things which choked the seed of God's word and prevented it being fruitful was 'the deceitfulness of riches' (Mk. 4: 19, AV).

The New Testament is utterly committed to the importance of heavenly treasure. Here the rich young ruler is told that, if he sells his goods and distributes to the poor, he will have treasure in heaven. In Luke 12 there is the rich farmer who is rebuilding his barns in order to be able to store more riches on earth, and we are told that this 'fool' represents those who are 'not rich toward God' (Lk. 12: 21). Then again, when Jesus was dining with a Pharisee one sabbath, He told him to give banquets to the poor and to people who could not invite him back, and that he would be rewarded at the resurrection of the just (Lk. 14: 12–14). It is the old issue: are we honest believers in supernaturalism, or not? Do we believe in a heaven, where accounts are kept and treasure can be stored, or not? Our hesitation about parting with earthly treasure is a measure of the reality of our belief at this point. If we really believe in God, and in heaven, and in the words of the Lord Jesus, we shall recognize the validity of heavenly treasure as a safe and gilt-edged investment!

Oddly enough, it is not only a test of our belief but also a proof of it, for our personal experience as a family has been that we have so far never been allowed to part with some substantial donation over and above our normal giving without it being abundantly returned from some other source and often multiplied into the bargain. So that, even down here, we seem to get our share of heavenly treasure too. God is no man's debtor. His giving to us (which is not to be measured merely on a financial scale) is always and evidently on a scale which makes our giving to Him seem utterly puny by comparison. This may perhaps be summed up very wonderfully in the familiar words, 'And my God will supply every need of yours according to his riches in glory in Christ Jesus' (Phil. 4: 19), on which a commentator has written: 'the rewarding will be not merely *from* His wealth, but also in a manner which befits His wealth—on a scale worthy of His wealth.'[5]

Our weak and doubting faith about heavenly treasure is helped and strengthened by that spilling over of His bounty which we experience here and now. The experience of men like Hudson Taylor and George Müller in the past, continuing into the present experience of the work which they founded, together with that of countless other Christians, should all help to strengthen our supernatural convictions.

[5] Quoted by R. P. Martin, *Philippians* (*Tyndale New Testament Commentaries*, Tyndale Press, 1959), p. 183.

Is tithing scriptural?

There is a common idea among Christians that God asks for a tenth, but the fact remains that in the New Testament Christians are nowhere urged to tithe. Ought we as Christians to tithe? There seem to be a number of ways in which this matter could be tackled. Mr Mitchell [6] lists the *compulsory contributions* which the people of God were supposed to give under the Old Covenant:

1. One-tenth of their income for the maintenance of the Levites.
2. One-tenth of their income for the festival purposes.
3. One-tenth of their income for the poor.
4. Wave Sheaves.
5. First-fruits.
6. Ungathered fruit left for the poor (gleaning).
7. Tithings of the increase of cattle and vines.
8. The cost of sacrifices and loss of time involved in worship at Jerusalem every three years.

He then goes on to suggest that *voluntary giving* began at this point, when they had already given at least a third of their income; such were the free-will offerings for the building of the Tabernacle and the Temple, to mention two outstanding 'appeals for funds' and the tremendous response to them.

It would take a great deal of very detailed comparison of texts one with another to sort this out, for while it is clear that the Israelites gave more than a simple tenth, what is not so clear is whether the same tithe was not described as being for different purposes at different times, being in any case multipurpose. It would be easy, for example, to refer to an interesting passage like Deuteronomy 14: 22–28: 'You shall tithe all the yield of your seed, which comes forth from the field year by year. And before the Lord your God, in the place which he will

6 *The Stewardship of Money* (IVF, 1951), p. 22.

'choose, to make his name dwell there, you shall eat the tithe of your grain, of your wine, and of your oil, and the firstlings of your herd and flock; that you may learn to fear the Lord your God always. And if the way is too long for you, so that you are not able to bring the tithe, when the Lord your God blesses you, because the place is too far from you . . . then you shall turn it into money . . . and spend the money for whatever you desire, oxen, or sheep, or wine or strong drink, whatever your appetite craves; and you shall eat there before the Lord your God and rejoice, you and your household. And you shall not forsake the Levite who is within your towns, for he has no portion or inheritance with you. At the end of every three years you shall bring forth all the tithe of your produce in the same year, and lay it up within your towns; and the Levite, because he has no portion or inheritance with you (*i.e.* no land of his own to cultivate and harvest), and the sojourner, the fatherless, and the widow, who are within your towns, shall come and eat and be filled; that the Lord your God may bless you in all the work of your hands that you do.'

This passage seems to show that the same tithe was used both for oneself, for the Levites and for the poor. Verse 26 suggests a kind of party in the Temple, when even strong drink was approved. Few of us have thought of applying our tithes in quite this way! It could also be argued that some of the tithes went for state taxes, because the priests and Levites performed some functions not unlike those of public health inspectors, a medical health service, and so on. In these days we do not count the paying of taxes to a secular state as part of our Christian giving, as they did in the days of a theocratic state. The principle of the tithe taken from the Old Testament certainly seems difficult to apply directly.

A second approach is to say that what was commanded under the law is only a shadow of what may be expected under grace, and that to niggle about proportions and to give the Lord a mere tenth shows a complete lack of understanding of the New Testament approach to giving. Actually in the Old Testament people gave according to their ability: 'Every man shall give as he is able, according to the blessing of the Lord your God which he has given you' (Dt. 16: 17); 'According to their ability they gave to the treasury' (Ezr. 2: 69); and this seems to be the principle which was continued in the New Testament: 'And the disciples determined, every one according to his ability, to send relief to the brethren who lived in Judea; and they did so . . .' (Acts 11: 29); 'On the first day of every week, each of you is to put something aside and store it up, as he may prosper' (or 'as God has prospered him') (1 Cor. 16: 2).

Actually New Testament references to tithing, of which there are some, seem to be mainly unfavourable. Thus the self-righteous Pharisee, comparing himself with others, says, 'I give tithes of all that I get' (Lk. 18: 12), and seems to regard this as one reason why he is justified before God. The other reference in the Gospels is where Jesus says, 'Woe to you Pharisees! for you tithe mint and rue and every herb, and neglect justice and the love of God; these you ought to have done, without neglecting the others' (Lk. 11: 42).

The Pharisees showed great attention to matters of detail, making sure that they gave an exact tenth, while ignoring some of the essential matters. Certainly in the Epistles Christians are never once urged to tithe, though they are urged to give. Christ commends the woman (Lk. 21: 1–4) who gave all that she had; nothing about tithing there. Paul writes about the generous giving of the Macedonians: 'their abundance of joy and their extreme poverty have overflowed in a wealth of liberality on their part. For they gave according to their means, as I can testify, and beyond their means, of their own free will . . . and this, not as we expected, but first they gave themselves to the Lord and to us by the will of God' (2 Cor. 8: 2–5).

This attitude does not seem to include any niggling ideas of proportions, and it is perhaps significant that, while Paul is dealing with giving both here (in chapters 8 and 9) and in other places, he nowhere mentions a tenth or any other fixed proportion. Someone talking of an address of Temple Gairdner's on the subject of 'Giving' said, 'I don't suppose any of the men who heard it ever again gave so little as a tenth. It sent me back to Oxford not only to pay my debts, but to live on half of what I had lived on before.' [7]

The slave owned no property absolutely; all the slave's belongings were really his master's. If we can develop the attitude that all we have is for Christ to use, how much better is it than the attitude 'I give a tenth, and the rest is mine'! If it is true that *we* are not our own, that we are bought with a price, it is also true of our possessions. It is easy to take the attitude that we will give such and such a proportion of our income to God, either setting it apart when our salary cheque comes in or when we get our pay packet, and then regarding our duty as done and the rest as ours to spend as we like. Of course it is a good thing, as a start, to set aside a regular proportion and if possible to increase it. But we want to use *all* our money in a way which is pleasing to God. Just as the tithers of old were told to buy what appealed to them in the way of food and drink, to share it with the Levite and with the poor and needy before the Lord, and were told to rejoice and enjoy it in His presence, so we may spend money and enjoy it, if it is done before the Lord. In all our spending and buying we need to ask ourselves: Is this purchase pleasing to God? This may not always mean the cheapest thing, for it may not be the best buy for the money. It is unlikely to be the most expensive thing either, for the *de luxe* article usually includes things we do not need. We have to be careful to avoid sheer self-indulgence or pride of dress or possession. A good test is the extent to which we want

[7] Quoted by Howard Guinness, *Sacrifice* (IVF, 1961), p. 14.

to show it off to other people or to gloat over it! In the
Old Testament one tribe in twelve, one day in seven and
one part in ten of income was thought of as belonging
especially to God. In the New Covenant we see all men as
holy, all days as those for pleasing God and all our income
to be used for Him.

Abstinence or extravagance?

One day at Whipsnade Zoo a party of young people were
thinking about refreshments and it was decided to buy
ice-creams. One person, however, refused. His thinking,
as he explained afterwards, was that we should steward
our money, and use as little as possible on ourselves. Ice-
cream is self-indulgence and just a luxury. 'I am a better
Christian than all these other people, who still have a
worldly approach to money. It's a shame that they should
be so blind to the need to be disciplined in these matters.'
This was probably true of some of the rest of us, but with
the party was an elderly saint, a returned missionary
and revered Bible teacher; there he was, with his clerical
hat brim tilted back, licking the remains of the ice-cream
off the paper with obvious, though undignified, enjoyment. Was he also a worldly and undisciplined Christian?
We knew he wasn't, and knew something of the frugality
of his home-life and the little economies of his daily living. But he was showing us that God has given us richly
all things to enjoy (1 Tim. 6: 17, AV) and, like the first
apostles, he was eating his food with joy and gladness
of heart.

It is not easy to strike the balance. Our determination
to be self-disciplined can lead us to be stingy, grudging
in opening our purses, counting the pennies, tight-fisted,
ungenerous. On the other hand our consciousness of
Christian liberty, of the great riches of the Lord in heaven,
or of the need for hospitality, may lead us to be wasteful,

ostentatious and secretly self-indulgent under the guise of generosity. God give us pure motives and joyous, care-free hearts which are able to give and go on giving, for 'It is more blessed to give than to receive' (Acts 20: 35).

Stewards

This idea of stewardship is a very helpful one. The *oikonomos* is the manager of a household or of household affairs, to whom the owner has entrusted the management of his affairs, the care of receipts and expenditures, and the duty of dealing out a proper portion to all the other members of the household.

This is a wonderful picture of the Christian and his responsibility. The Lord has entrusted to us certain goods, for the blessing of the household at large, including, of course, our own needs. We are to dispense them to others on His behalf. They are His goods and we are answerable to Him for the way in which we distribute them. If we are extravagant on ourselves and purse-pinching with others, then there will be a reckoning when the Master returns (Lk. 12: 42–48; 16: 1, 2). We may list the duties:

1. He was entrusted with his Master's goods.
2. He was to use them for the household.
3. He himself was also provided for, but not at the expense of others.
4. He had to be prudent and plan his outlay, not using up in a day what was meant for a month. Nor was he to hang on to money that he was meant to be spending.
5. He had to give an account of what he had done with his Master's goods.

One knows Christian stewards who fulfil their office. You visit them and you come away with some book, which they thought you might like and find helpful. A cheque arrives, because they knew that with so much sickness in the family you would need some help. They have a small cottage by the sea and it happens to be vacant, and they wondered if . . . (the fact that they could probably rent it to someone else for a large sum is, to them, beside the point). They happen to have a free evening and wondered if you would like them to mind the children for you so that you can go out together. They wondered if your boy would like to go to camp to keep their boy company. They know you have been busy recently and they just happened to be baking, and they probably do not taste very nice (for the Westerner can be as self-deprecating as any Oriental when he chooses), but please do take them. They happen to have an old pram, high chair, cot, play-pen, refrigerator, stove, *etc.*, and they don't need them any more . . . The fact that they are in lovely condition and might be offered for sale is irrelevant to them, it seems.

These are the Lord's good stewards whose love and generosity bring sweetness and joy with their goods. They always seem to be taking thought for other people and their needs and circumstances: what can they possibly do to help? Their home is open to the homeless, their ear to the distressed who want someone to share their distress, their table can always take a few extra people, their car always leaves early for church to pick up the sick or the elderly on the way and take them home again afterwards. This is what it means to be a steward. Is it only a coincidence that their neighbours seem so ready to become Christians also?

Students often have less of this world's goods to be generous with than other people, and it may more often be a matter of generous lending than generous giving. 'Do not withhold good from those to whom it is due, when it is in your power to do it. Do not say to your neighbour, "Go, and come again, tomorrow I will give it"—when you have it with you' (Pr. 3: 27, 28). It is easy to take a dog-in-the-manger attitude about loaning one's own things, textbooks and the like, the more so when the fear that it may not be returned either soon or in one piece may have some foundation. There is still plenty of room for generosity in a student context. The author can never forget visiting a country which materially was very poor, and being moved to tears by the generosity of students in producing little farewell gifts, perhaps a small souvenir or hand-painted card, of no great monetary value, and yet indicative of Christian love and brotherhood.

There are, of course, other attitudes. Some of us tremble lest we are always the takers and only too rarely the givers. Somehow we don't think, or take thought, until it is too late. We fail to take thought for others in the household, because we are so very busy with our own personal concerns. And some don't wish to be givers or takers: 'We don't want to be indebted to anybody, and we don't want them to bother with us and we don't want to have to bother with them.' The money lies in the bank unused, except when we want a larger car. The drawers remain full of goods for which we have little use, the beautiful guest-rooms lie clean and spotless, the furniture retains its lovely polish, for no energetic children are ever allowed to disturb the placid beauty of the home! How useless is unused money, how pointless are unpossessed possessions. God give us grace to be proper stewards.

Systematic giving

Because of our own frailty it does seem important that we should settle for a basic proportionate giving, and then give more than that whenever there is some clear opportunity. Fix on some proportion. For the very poor (and so often these are the dear people who give so much. The missionary societies often receive gifts from aging people; it may not seem a large gift, but often it represents a great deal of scraping and saving) even a tenth may be too much. For the very rich it is certainly far too little. We all do well to review the proportion of our giving. Am I missing it at all? Is it putting any curb at all on my other spending? If not, then it may be well prayerfully to increase the proportion. If 20% does not hurt much, then push it up a bit and see how much you can give, and never tell anyone.

Clearly this fixing of a proportion depends on the rate of taxation, your responsibilities and so on. A single person with no family responsibilities and no relations to support can give more. A student who is earning nothing, but getting support from the government or his family, is in a different position to a wage-earner. What we give may be from salary, wages, dividends, scholarships, gifts, pocket money.

Fix, then, on a regular amount. Use it thoughtfully and prayerfully. It can be a good exercise. So much to one's local church, so much to a missionary society (home, foreign, or both), so much to a particular needy person, or perhaps to Christian broadcasting, literature or medical work. It may vary from month to month, quarter to quarter and year to year. A sudden urgent need may make us want to make an additional 'free-will offering', something which costs, which we anticipate will make us postpone the purchase of some long-desired personal item or surrender some luxury. It is a question of how much we give and not how little. Wesley's injunction retains its force, 'Get all you can. Save all you can. Give all you can.' The Master who entrusts us with possessions and money commands us to use them, not hoard them, only we are to use them for His glory and for the blessing of our fellow men.

Suggestions for prayer and meditation

As a servant of Jesus Christ, do I recognize His claim on all I possess?

Am I a steward of my possessions in using them for others, or only for my own selfish enjoyment? Is there some practical way I can remedy this at once?

Do I just drop something into the collection plate when it is offered, or do I plan to give a regular amount, and distribute this thoughtfully and intelligently?

Am I in danger of becoming rather mean in self-discipline over money?

Do I have a real joy in living for God and giving for God?

What causes are there for which I might covenant to give regularly?

'On the first day of every week, each of you is to put something aside and store it up, as he may prosper, so that contributions need not be made when I come' (1 Cor. 16: 2).

'Now as you excel in everything—in faith, in utterance, in knowledge, in all earnestness, and in your love for us —see that you excel in this gracious work also' (2 Cor. 8: 7).

5 PREJUDICE or CONVICTION?

*Take my intellect, and use
Every power as Thou shalt choose.*

When asked which commandment of the law is the most important, the Lord Jesus replies that it is to 'love the Lord your God with all your heart, and with all your soul, and with all your mind (Gk. *dianoia*), and with all your strength' (Mk. 12: 30). When the scribe replies (verse 33) he says 'to love him with all the heart, and with all the understanding', and paraphrasing uses another word (Gk. *sunesis*). This is the word which means 'the faculty of comprehension, intelligence, acuteness, shrewdness' and is the word used when the young Jesus is listening and asking questions of the doctors in the Temple, and all who heard Him were amazed at His 'understanding' (Lk. 2: 47).

We are to love God with *all* our mind, with all our intellect. It is not enough that we have a religious compartment in our thinking. The whole mind is to be given to Him for His service. We are to think about our faith and about its application. There can be no excuse for intellectual sloth. We are to think in order that we may grapple with the thinking of others, including those who are antagonists of the Christian faith, to the utmost of our ability. It needs to be made clear that faith is not some more respectable religious name for prejudice or superstition. We need to be those with a deep concern for truth; not only for that truth which has been divinely revealed, but also that which God has left for man to discover for himself. Over the gate of the Cavendish Laboratory in Cambridge we may read the words: 'The works of the Lord are great, sought out of all them that have pleasure therein' (Ps. 111: 2). We need to exult in true knowledge about the universe.

We must give our minds to the Lord for Him to use so that we may understand and explain Christian truth to others, so that we may challenge shoddy or illogical thinking among Christians, and so that we may rejoice in the truth. It is nonsense to suggest that to become a Christian means to surrender one's critical faculties.

Monica Furlong, speaking of the collapse of organized religion, and the holocaust sweeping away the bric-à-brac of institutional religion, writes enthusiastically: 'What seems clear is that within all the denominations there is a new mutation of Christian (as yet only faintly discernible from the inert mass) who is willing and eager to question every item of his faith, who is bored to death with the old clichés, the old humbug and the great herd of sacred cows, and who believes that to disable either his mind or his senses is to dishonour Christ.' [1]

It is interesting to notice the word mutation, and the suggestion that until comparatively recently Christians have been content to be sacred cowherds willing to disable their minds. As we shall see, if not a mutation, at least a metamorphosis in thinking has always been required of Christians.

Of course we should think. What is so absurd is the suggestion that those in favour of 'religionless' Christianity and a secularized rethinking of faith have been the only people to be urging thought. For from exactly the opposite viewpoint we get Harry Blamires writing: 'Except over a very narrow field of thinking, chiefly touching questions of strictly personal conduct, we Christians in the modern world accept, for the purpose of mental

[1] *Manchester Guardian*, 11 January 1963.

activity, a frame of reference constructed by the secular mind and a set of criteria reflecting secular evaluations. There is no Christian mind . . .'[2] Of course Christians must think; but it must be with a Christian mind.

The non-Christian mind

Very few popular writers about 'the rubble of Christendom', and so forth, seem to have taken the trouble to understand or to give full weight to what the Bible says about non-Christian minds. The Bible insists upon a revolution in thinking because it has a very dark view of the condition of the mind of man who disregards God. Thus, 'although they knew God they did not honour him as God or give thanks to him, but they became futile in their thinking and their senseless minds were darkened' (Rom. 1: 21); and again, 'God gave them up to a base mind' (lit. 'a mind void of judgment') (Rom. 1: 28); or again, 'the carnal mind is enmity against God' (Rom. 8: 7, AV); and again, 'and you who once were estranged and hostile in mind' (Col. 1: 21); and 'the god of this world has blinded the minds of the unbelievers' (2 Cor. 4: 4); and 'they are darkened in their understanding, alienated from the life of God because of the ignorance that is in them, due to their hardness of heart' (Eph. 4: 18).

Now the purpose of all these quotations is not only to show that this is no isolated teaching, but also to show that from a Christian point of view the very fact of becoming a Christian demands that there be a new kind of thinking. We must think; and, significantly, we must think differently from the way we used to think.

This point is perhaps underlined by the word used in the New Testament which means literally a change of mind, or a change of thinking (Gk. *metanoia*), seeing things in a new way. This is the word which we translate

[2] H. Blamires, *The Christian Mind* (SPCK, 1963), p. 4.

as 'repentance'. In order to become a Christian you must have a change of mind, a new way of thinking. All this underlines that to be a real Christian must mean to love God with all the mind, the intellect or the intelligence.

The non-conforming mind

In the Old Testament (Je. 31: 31–34) God promised that under the New Covenant He would put his laws into their minds (Heb. 8: 10) or write them on their minds (Heb. 10: 16). In the same passage which spoke of the alienated and darkened minds, Christians are urged to 'be renewed in the spirit of your minds' (Eph. 4: 23), and in another place Paul writes: 'Do not be conformed to this world but be transformed by the renewal of your mind, that you may prove what is the will of God . . .' (Rom. 12: 2). The word for 'transform' in Greek is *metamorphoō*; there must be a change, a metamorphosis or transfiguration (the same word is used for the transfiguration of Christ).

This transformation is contrasted with conformation to the world. It is rather difficult to recognize in this contrast any possible support for the idea of the secularization of Christianity. The Bible appears to be asking for desecularization. The last thing the Christian must do is conform to the secular society. There must be a revolution in thinking. We must be 'willing and eager to question every item' of the old thinking; there can be secular cows as well as sacred cows. The word for 'conforming' has the idea of following the fashion of something. There is little doubt that the world in general goes in for conformity, and in these days of television the pressure of mass advertising seems to mean that more and more people wear the same clothes, and decorate their almost identical apartments in an almost identical manner, and so on. The Christian is a man who questions fashions and refuses to conform. He has a different norm. His norm is not, or should not be, what everybody else does. In his thinking, it is not what everybody else thinks. His norm must not even be set by a thoughtless conformity to the behaviour of those in the churches. He may on occasion differ from them if he is determined to follow the biblical norm.

The Christian is not a nonconformist just for its own sake, any more than Christ was.[3] There have always been Bohemians determined to be different and in rebellion against the drab uniformity of conforming society. The Christian has some sympathy with such people; he too is called to be different, he is called to question the sheep-like behaviour of the crowd, but for rather different reasons. He is not in rebellion against society, but seeking to conform to the will of God, against whom society is in rebellion. He has no desire to make himself conspicuous, and sees no value in being odd for its own sake, and while some human fashions are rather silly, it would be equally silly to cling to the fashions of a former generation. The new look is only different from the old, not necessarily worse or better. The mind of the Christian has to be continually exercised about when to protest and when not. He cannot become a kind of permanent niggler for whom nothing is right. You cannot take issue with everything, but must decide when a protest is in order. At the same time he knows his natural tendency to conform and be cowardly, to try to avoid being different.

'What is one to do? For on the one hand, quite certainly, there is a degree of unprotesting participation in such talk which is very bad. We are strengthening the hand of the enemy. We are encouraging them to believe that "those Christians", once you get them off their guard and round a dinner table, really think and feel exactly as he does. By implication we are denying our Master; behaving as if we "knew not the Man". On the other hand

[3] See p. 22 above.

is one to show that, like Queen Victoria, one is "not amused"? Is one to be contentious, interrupting the flow of conversation at every moment with "I don't agree. I don't agree"? Or rise and go away? But by these courses we may also confirm some of their worst suspicions of "those Christians". We are just the sort of ill-mannered prigs they always said.' [4]

It is far from easy to be a nonconformist. We shall certainly sometimes not be able to avoid giving offence. Lord, give us grace to see where we cannot conform to accepted custom, and to question accepted ideas pointedly, without being priggish.

The source of knowledge of God

Perhaps the best introduction to this is a characteristic quotation from Blamires: 'A tragic aspect of all this is that outsiders think of the noisy rebellious heretics as representative of the Church. The public hear fallacious deviations from orthodoxy uttered by clergy in the Press or on the air, and imagine that theirs is the Church's teaching. Off-centre clergy often acquire neatly devised techniques of passing themselves off as being in the swim or in the know. "Of course the best Anglican scholarship today would hold that . . . Of course most up-to-date Christian thinkers have come round to the view that . . ." The effect of gambits like these, unsubtle as they may appear to the cunning mind, can be potent on the untrained mind. Some of the insidious implications they convey are worth analysing. One is the pernicious notion that, in theology, amendments are continually being made by a kind of democratic committee procedure carried out among a lot of learned men (whom you and I would scarcely by able to understand, but with whom the speaker by good fortune happens to be on familiar

[4] C. S. Lewis, *Reflections on the Psalms* (Bles, 1958), p. 63.

terms). Another false implication is that established Christian truth is more or less non-existent. There is only a mass of individual opinions, which sometimes agree together in sufficient numbers to produce a probable proposition.' [5]

This makes clear a very commonly held confusion about Christian truth, that it is only some old tradition anyhow and can easily be changed. One rather suspects that this is what Monica Furlong means by questioning 'every item of his faith'.

We can see the sun only in its own light. The only knowledge we have of God is what God has revealed to us. What we know about God is not a lot of guesswork by a few religious thinkers, but what God has chosen to reveal to us. We know next to nothing about the stranger who remains obstinately silent. It is only when he 'opens up' and begins to talk about himself that we know very much about him. Unless God has spoken, then we can know next to nothing about Him. The Christian faith exists only because God has spoken in history, through Moses and the prophets and then supremely in Christ. Apart from this revelation we know nothing about God, and we have no authority to make 'amendments' to the content of the Christian faith. This does not mean, however, that faith is a kind of excrescence added on as a kind of extra faculty and completely divorced from reason. While natural, unenlightened, human reason cannot arrive at knowledge of God, when God has revealed Himself, what He reveals proves to be quite consonant with reason. It has a 'fitness' about it. Indeed reason is essential to its proper understanding. 'The benefit of nature's light must not be thought excluded as unnecessary, because the necessity of a diviner light is magnified.'[6]

The Christian mind must be prepared to grapple with non-Christian thinking. The more intelligent type of

[5] H. Blamires, *The Christian Mind* (SPCK, 1963), p. 129.
[6] Richard Hooker, *Ecclesiastical Polity*, chapter 14.

unbeliever is not impressed by the kind of gospel presentation which ignores objections, skirts difficulties and then, having stressed that people are not converted by reason, makes a sustained attempt to convert them by emotion instead! The unbeliever needs to know that you recognize an objection, and can answer it at least to your own satisfaction, and that while in some area you admit a difficulty for faith, you can show a greater difficulty for unbelief. We owe it to non-Christians to deal honestly with their genuine difficulties,[7] and not politely to ignore them, or brush them aside with a reference to the darkness of unenlightened minds. And when one cannot answer, the Christian has to resist the temptation to try to win the argument willy-nilly—for then my winning the argument has become more important than the Lord winning the man—and by exercise of Christian integrity and humility admit that I do not know the answer . . . but will take steps to find out. Nothing is to be gained from blustering on or taking what both you and the other fellow know to be an evasion of the real question at issue.

Just as the Lord Jesus opened the minds of His disciples 'to understand the scriptures' (Lk. 24: 45), so the Holy Spirit enlightens the mind to understand revelation. 'No one comprehends the thoughts of God except the Spirit of God. Now we have received . . . the Spirit . . ., that we might understand the gifts bestowed on us by God. And we impart this in words not taught by human wisdom but taught by the Spirit, interpreting spiritual truths to those who possess the Spirit. The natural man does not receive the gifts of the Spirit of God, for they are folly to him, and he is not able to understand them because they are spiritually discerned' (1 Cor. 2: 11–14). The Bible view

[7] One is not referring to the smokescreen of bogus and second-hand objections, the old chestnuts that people churn out with heartfelt insincerity when conversation touches on personal issues and the Christian arguments begin to sound frighteningly relevant.

of the inadequacy of the unenlightened human reason
may not be a popular one, but it accords with experience
and, moreover, with reason. 'We must remember that its
(the Bible's) message for us can be understood only by
means of a "divine light". Biblical faith offers us categories by which we may interpret and understand the
world and its history and lives in their relation to God,
and it is uncompromisingly opposed to all forms of rationalism—the view that the human reason is, in view of
its own inherent perfection, a competent and impartial judge of truth and falsehood in all matters, whether
secular or religious. In the popular mind today, and in a
good deal of popular Christianity, this type of rationalism
still persists, a hangover from the eighteenth century, and
the very essence of "the liberal illusion": even those
"advanced" thinkers who boast of their acquaintance
with Marx and Freud still trust in themselves that they
are rational and despise others. The idea of an impartial
abstract reason is a mirage, a notable illustration of man's
perennial temptation to exalt himself among the gods,
knowing good and evil. Our reason is, as we have noted
in previous contexts, "conditioned" by many things such
as education, environment, class position and so on. In
fact, unless it is thus conditioned, that is supplied with
categories from outside itself, reason cannot function at
all . . .'[8]

For the Christian mind, or reason, this education is
the education of the Holy Spirit and the environment
that of the people of God. This is the 'conditioning' we
need if we are to arrive at an understanding of Christian
truth. This is what the New Testament says: 'We have
not ceased to pray for you, asking that you may be filled
with the knowledge of his will in all spiritual wisdom and
understanding . . .' (Col. 1: 9); 'to have all the riches of
assured understanding and the knowledge of God's

[8] Alan Richardson, *Christian Apologetics* (SCM Press, 1947), p.
223.

mystery, of Christ, in whom are hid all the treasures of wisdom and knowledge' (Col. 2: 2, 3).

Christians must think

The New Testament is full of exhortations to Christians to think. The possession of God's revelation in the Bible, and of the Holy Spirit to interpret, does not relieve us of the responsibility to think (any more than the possession of a copy of the score and the presence of the conductor on the rostrum relieve the member of the orchestra of the responsibility to play his instrument with all the skill that he can). Otherwise the New Testament would not be full of exhortations to think, such as: 'Brethren, do not be children in your thinking; be babes in evil, but in thinking be mature' (1 Cor. 14: 20); 'Think over what I say, for the Lord will grant you understanding in everything' (2 Tim. 2: 7); 'Gird up your minds' (1 Pet. 1: 13). There is to be a mental awakening, a fresh outburst of mental activity. The writer to the Hebrews scolds them because, when by this time they ought to be teachers, they need to be instructed all over again in the first principles of the faith (Heb. 5: 12). There can be no excuse for intellectual sloth. We must be certain that what we hold are reasoned convictions, and not blind prejudices.

The Christian mind must grapple with things which are a problem to faith. Difficulties will not be merely ignored, but honestly faced and answered. We may need the help of other Christians to do it, but think them through we must. This is involved in loving the Lord with all our mind. Often the answer to some criticisms is not a categorical denial or refutation. We are not to defend the Christian church or its members right or wrong. It is here that we are right to question institutionalism and the medieval bric-à-brac which some churches have succeeded in accumulating to the extent of becoming more like museums than anything else.

For example, suppose we are met with an attack on methods of Christian evangelism as a kind of emotional brain-washing, taking advantage of adolescents' insecurity to pressure them through an emotional crisis into the Christian church. 'Conversion is nothing but a kind of psychological technique.' Our first reaction may be to defend the doctrine of conversion and the church's methods. But we have to admit that in some cases this may be a fair criticism and that some evangelism is getting extraordinarily near to this caricature. Some so-called conversions may be 'no more' than this. But this does not overthrow the validity of genuine conversions, nor is it true that all conversions occur in adolescence, or in the type of meeting that is described. Nor is it necessary to carry out evangelism in that way in order to get results; indeed, knowing the danger, we shall be careful to do all we can to avoid that kind of spurious profession of faith, which is due to human persuasion or pressure technique rather than to the working of the Spirit of God. We have no brief to defend things in the churches which are a departure from what God has revealed to us in the Bible. Indeed these are the things which we ourselves must question.

It is a very thrilling thing to see the way in which some Christians have been obedient to these commands to think. They have dared to differ with some very commonly held interpretation because it did not seem consistent with the rest of the Bible. Young William Carey, living in a generation when there were no missionary meetings or missionary concern, pins up a map of the world in his workshop over his shoemaker's bench, and seeks to find out all he can about the non-Christian world. In his day everybody understood the command to go into all the world, and to make disciples of all nations, as applying only to the first apostles. Calvin, Luther and, indeed, apparently all the Reformers had taken this view. Carey observed that the promise in the following verse continued to the close of the age, so why not the command? 'Go therefore and make disciples of all nations, baptizing them in the name of the Father and of the Son and of the Holy Spirit, teaching them to observe all that I have commanded you; and lo, I am with you always, to the close of the age' (Mt. 28: 19, 20). When he dared to suggest that perhaps the command also applied to the end of the age, he was told: 'Young man, sit down. When God wishes to convert the heathen he will do it without your help or mine.' This was the prevailing viewpoint of that time; but Carey persisted that teaching others to observe *all* Christ's commands must, at the very least, include passing on this very command to go and make disciples of all nations. Even the Reformers could be wrong! They too were fallible men, and Carey was able to prove his point by the use of enlightened Christian reasoning about the words of Scripture itself.

Christians may differ

We have just seen that, while the Bible may be infallible, Christians certainly are not, and we need to be very careful not to suggest that an infallible Bible means that we have infallible interpretations. Ought Christians to differ from each other and should we not expect a common mind? Many quote: 'I appeal to you, brethren, by the name of our Lord Jesus Christ, that all of you agree and that there be no dissensions among you, but that you be united in the same mind and the same judgment' (1 Cor. 1: 10); and I have even heard this used as a lever to insist that therefore *you* must agree with *my* interpretation. The Bible says you must!

However, we have to take this passage in the light of other passages also. For example: 'Let every one be fully convinced in his own mind' (Rom. 14: 5) is in the con-

text of Christians having different views about the observ-
ing of festival days, or about the kind of food they should
eat. We know from elsewhere that Paul himself has extremely strong convictions on both these subjects (Gal.
4: 10; 1 Cor. 8: 13), but here he tells people to make
up their own minds without making it a reason for criticism, dissension or a break of fellowship.

Moreover, in the letter to the Galatians we can see how
first the men who came from James, and then Peter, and
then the rest of the Jews, and then Barnabas, all with-
drew from eating with the Gentiles (Gal. 2: 12–14).
Only Paul was prepared to stand out against this and to
show how wrong it was. Even leading apostles could be
in error and misunderstand crucial issues. Just as Christians are not free from all indwelling sin from the
moment of conversion, but it lingers on, so they are not
free from indwelling error. Both morally and intellectually they are still able to err, and do err. God permits
this. Certainly one way in which we grow in maturity is
by battling with sin and battling with error: there seems
to be some purpose for which we are allowed to be vague
on certain matters—in order perhaps to make us think.
Had it been His will, He could have included in the
Bible such instructions about the subjects and the mode
of baptism or about church order which would have
placed them out of the realm of controversy; but God has
not chosen to do this. There is thus forced upon us the
necessity to think and reason about the meaning of certain passages. We have to distinguish between what the
Bible actually says and what we think it says, and perhaps be delivered from some set misconception based on
some talk that we once heard. We have to take clear note
of the context of biblical statements, and see when an
argument from silence may have validity and when it
need have none. There is always this danger, that we hold
certain views from mere prejudice, and not with genuine
conviction.

The limitations of the Christian mind

It seems important also, in this same respect, that we be prepared to be perfectly frank about the things we do not know. There are plenty of indications within the New Testament about the limitations on the knowledge of Christian men. We are told that God 'is able to do far more abundantly than all that we ask or think' (Eph. 3: 20) and that the peace of God passes all power of thought (Phil. 4: 7), while in the well-known chapter on love our present knowledge is identified with that of a child, compared with the adult knowledge we shall one day have, when we no longer see through a glass darkly (1 Cor. 13: 9-12). Paul says specifically that our knowledge is imperfect and that now we know only in part. This should deliver us from becoming over-dogmatic upon matters which are not clear in the Bible. In the case of some problems we have to confess that we do not know and that we are baffled by them. If we do this we shall be in good company, for, after dealing with the ever problematical relationships between divine sovereignty and human responsibility, Paul can only burst into a doxology: 'O the depth of the riches and wisdom and knowledge of God! How unsearchable are his judgments and how inscrutable his ways! "For who has known the mind of the Lord, or who has been his counsellor? Or who has given a gift to him that he might be repaid?" For from him and through him and to him are all things. To him be glory for ever. Amen' (Rom. 11: 33-36).

We must all recognize the limitations upon our human understanding. Like Paul we can only bow ourselves in praise before the great mind of God. It certainly helps us to get our own puny thinking in perspective.

A necessary warning

'Trust in the Lord with all your heart, and do not rely on your own insight. In all your ways acknowledge him, and he will make straight your paths. Be not wise in your own eyes . . .' (Pr. 3: 5ff.). There is a danger in intellectual self-confidence, if we think that we can look after ourselves and think our way through any problem. It is this spirit in the unbeliever which is the very essence of sin, and there is always a danger that it may become the sin of the Christian intellectual, even of the theological intellectual. We may have a God-centred theology, which is peculiarly dependent upon human argumentation, and where in daily attitude we are still not really depending on the Lord with *all* our hearts or acknowledging Him in *all* our ways. Our faith can become an arid intellectual exercise. 'And if I . . . understand all mysteries and all knowledge . . ., but have not love, I am nothing' (1 Cor. 13: 2). There can be a danger for the man who is too self-consciously intellectual. There is a danger that we may not really have surrendered our intellect to the Lord at all, but are thinking independently of God's illumination, leaning on our own understanding.

It is Paul who wrote of the danger of having knowledge without love, and he was a man of considerable intellectual ability. Yet he writes of 'the foolishness of preaching' (1 Cor. 1: 21, AV) and of the danger that men's faith may stand only in 'the plausible words of (man's) wisdom' (1 Cor. 2: 4) instead of in the power of God. It is this same man who speaks of the confidence which he might have had in the flesh, but which he counts as loss and refuse 'because of the surpassing worth of knowing Christ Jesus my Lord' (Phil. 3: 4–8). Paul would urge us to depend upon the Lord and not upon our own insight or understanding.

'Take my intellect,' prays Frances Havergal. There is a

real danger that the Christian may be orthodox in 'belief' or 'doctrine' and yet not surrender his intellect for the Master's use. The intellect too must be sanctified, set apart for the service of God. This does not mean that it is to be ignored, suppressed by some form of intellectual dishonesty; but rather that it finds its fullest freedom and expression in dependence upon God, the Fount of all reason and truth, in whom are hid all the treasures of wisdom and knowledge.

Intellect or wisdom?

Some of us lack in the intellectual realm; our IQ is no more than average. But it is not only great intellects who are commanded to love the Lord with all their mind. All men have minds. They may be one-, two- or five-talent minds, but we are still expected to invest our intellectual capital for the glory of God. Even a one-talent mind can be developed by use, and we are taught that it must be.

Again and again the Bible reminds us that wisdom is to be sought from God. 'Yes, if you cry out for insight and raise your voice for understanding, if you seek it like silver and search for it as for hidden treasures; then you will understand the fear of the Lord and find the knowledge of God. For the Lord gives wisdom; from his mouth come knowledge and understanding' (Pr. 2: 3–6). This is perfectly plain, that God is the Source of all wisdom. Solomon himself asked for this wisdom (1 Ki. 3: 9–12) and this man plainly told others that this wisdom of his, a wisdom which has become proverbial, this 'wise and discerning mind', was a gift from God.

The teaching of the New Testament is the same. 'If any of you lacks wisdom, let him ask God who gives to all men generously and without reproaching, and it will be given him' (Jas. 1: 5). We are told that all the treasures of wisdom and knowledge are hidden in Christ (Col. 2: 3)

101

and that of God He is made unto us wisdom (1 Cor. 1: 30, AV). In the list of spiritual gifts we are told that to some the Spirit gives 'the utterance of wisdom' and to others 'the utterance of knowledge according to the same Spirit' (1 Cor. 12: 8). If these are spiritual gifts, then they are not meted out once and for all at birth; but those who lack them, and would exercise such gifts, are urged earnestly to desire them (1 Cor. 12: 31; 14: 1), for, like other spiritual gifts, they may be sought from God.

It really is astonishing sometimes how people, whom one would think, humanly speaking, were not at all promising, suddenly blossom out with one or more spiritual gifts. It is almost as though the Lord wants to show His power and what He can do to confute our low opinion of one of His children. He is the Giver, the great Giver, and He gives gifts to men, and though it is right for us to esteem others better than ourselves, and seek to make a sober assessment of what gifts we do and do not have, He has told us to *ask* for wisdom and to seek earnestly the best gifts. Why do we delay?

The intellect in action

Somehow the Philippian Epistle, as we have seen already and will see again, seems to epitomize something of the whole-hearted passion for Christ and His service of which we are trying to write. It is therefore interesting to see the points at which Paul sees a consecrated intellect as essential for his Philippian converts.

Their love is to abound more and more, but it is to be tempered by 'knowledge and all discernment' (and the word in Greek here is *aisthēsis*, presumably related to our word aesthetic), 'so that you may approve what is excellent . . .' (Phil. 1: 9, 10). Here is a warm and abounding love, which is not sentimental or foolish, but is qualified by these intellectual qualities. We are to love with all our mind.

They are to have the humble mind which characterized the Lord with a divine intellect, who yet was willing to take the form of a Servant (Phil. 2: 5–7). It seems clear that, in the matter of sanctification and holiness, there is some difference of view between them. Paul has stressed that what matters is progress in perfection, always straining for further advance (Phil. 3: 12); whereas those who say they are already perfect tend to be satisfied with where they have got to, while those who think perfection is not possible in this life have stopped trying. Neither one is moving forward at all. Paul says both views are wrong, as they are content with stationary sanctification, with where they are already; so he writes: 'Let those of us who are mature be thus minded; and if in anything you are otherwise minded, God will reveal that also to you' (Phil. 3: 15). There may be differences of view, but let us wait on God for further understanding.

He reminds the Philippians that the peace of God, which is beyond the capacity of human intellect to grasp fully, will yet guard and keep their hearts and their minds in Christ Jesus (Phil. 4: 7), and this presumably because they are not to have anxiety about anything (even intellectual problems?), but to pray over it. That is when the peace of God is promised. The anxious, prayerless intellect may not enjoy that peace.

Finally, there is the glorious exhortation prefaced by his second 'Finally': 'whatever is true, whatever is honourable, whatever is just, whatever is pure, whatever is lovely, whatever is gracious, if there is any excellence, if there is anything worthy of praise, *think* about these things' (Phil. 4: 8). And what better exhortation could there be to the Christian mind, to the consecrated intellect, than that? What better occupation for that mind, and what better note on which to close this chapter?

Suggestions for prayer and meditation

Am I a thoughtful Christian, or is my faith in a water-tight compartment, kept separate and apart from my intellectual life?

Am I slavishly following the norm of what is usually done, or thinking out my behaviour again from biblical principles?

How far has there been an intellectual revolution since I was converted, or do I still have the same old humanistic, man-centred thought-patterns?

Am I thinking and exercising my mind with books that challenge my thinking, or merely reading light literature for relaxation?

Do I merely argue with non-Christians, or can I challenge their thinking in a thought-provoking way in order to point them to Christ?

Are my doctrinal beliefs and church practices merely inherited prejudices or genuine convictions?

Am I in danger of intellectual pride, despising others, and cold in heart and lacking the indispensable Christian love?

Do I think about what is true, honourable, just, pure, lovely, gracious, excellent and worthy of praise—or do I waste time with what is not these things?

Am I really serving my Lord with *all* my mind?

6

ROMANCE
or LOVE?

Take my love; my Lord, I pour
At Thy feet its treasure-store.

All of us have a capacity for love stored up in our hearts like an alabaster box of fragrant ointment. Is it to be selfishly locked up, hoarded for secret appropriation, or is it to be lavishly poured out so that human society may be filled with the fragrance of the ointment? (See Jn. 12: 3.) What are we to do with this precious thing, this desire to love and be loved; how shall it be used? To use a less romantic and more contemporary analogy, there is a tremendous potential in this human capacity for love, blessing and energy waiting to be released; but how shall it be used? Just as nuclear energy may have tremendous potential for good and for evil, so also does this emotional energy have great potential for both good and evil. How is it to be controlled and its use directed into paths of joy and blessing? Love is something which all men and women have to give, and which all want to receive, at all stages of life. The child needs it, and so does the adult, and very often it is the very old who feel most their lack of it. The inexplicable thing is that, when all have it to give, and all want to receive, there should still be such a scarcity of it.

What do we mean by love? The words seems rather over-worked in an attempt to describe the nature of God or of Christian experience, and it is often in this context very vague and ambiguous. It tries to express the inexpressible, but fails to do it. The word is used in so many senses: self-love, parental love, sexual love, brotherly love, love for mankind, and so on.

Christian love

The Bible seems to see love as something which ought to be particularly a characteristic of Christians. There is even a revolution in grammar entailed in the 'change of mind' involved in becoming a Christian. For we naturally speak egocentrically of 'I' as the first person singular, and seem to find no difficulty in relating this grammar with experience. The other fellow falls into place as the second person, while the third person is he, she or it. But in Hebrew grammar we meet an interesting reversal in that the first person refers to 'him', the second to 'you', and I myself have dropped back into third person. It has been natural for us to think of ourselves as first, and God has come a poor third, if anywhere in our thinking; but since we have changed our minds there has been a revolution and we now recognize that God is the first person in our lives. Thus the first commandment was summed up by Christ as loving the Lord our God with all our heart, all our soul, all our mind and all our strength (Mk. 12: 30). The second commandment relates to the second person and tells me that I should love my neighbour as myself (Mk. 12: 31), and that from now on, instead of putting my own interests first, I must put the interests of others at least on a level with my own. (This is, of course, much easier to write or to give assent to than it is actually to follow in practice.)

The Bible then establishes a new set of priorities for our love. The word comes again and again; for example, it is used no less than seventeen times, either as verb or noun, in the letter to the Ephesians. In other places one meets with those fascinating compounds: *philadelphia*, 'love of the brethren' (1 Pet. 1: 22) or 'brotherly love' (Rom. 12: 10, AV); *philostorgos*, love of family or 'kindly affectioned' (Rom. 12: 10, AV); *philoxenos*, love of strangers or 'hospitality' (Rom. 12: 13); while in Titus 2: 4 one finds *philandros* and *philoteknos*, loving one's husband and children. Christians are to love like brothers, like members of the same family.

This is because God first loved us (1 Jn. 4: 10). Our love is called forth in response to Him, who loved me and gave Himself for me (Gal. 2: 20). 'Therefore be imitators of God, as beloved children. And walk in love, as Christ loved us and gave himself up for us, a fragrant offering and sacrifice to God' (Eph. 5: 1, 2). Here we get the idea of the fragrance of the love of Christ poured out, and it is our response to this love of Christ, and to the fact that we are 'beloved' of God, which is the rationale behind the command that we should walk in love. Perhaps the most wonderful passage on this is in Romans 5, where we are told that 'God's love has been poured into our hearts through the Holy Spirit which has been given to us' (Rom 5: 5). In the following verses we can see that, while we men choose to love that which is lovely or lovable or which loves us in return, the love of God is astonishingly different because it is expressed to those who are sinners (verse 8), who are lacking in moral strength and are ungodly (verse 6), and who are even His enemies (verse 10). God's love is extended to those who are totally unworthy to be the recipients of it, who in His sight are defiled, corrupt, lacking moral fibre, and who are hostile and defiant towards Him. Christian love, then, is the response of a heart overwhelmed with a sense of its own unworthiness and contamination with sin and selfish motives, and yet a heart which finds that, although God knows all this about us, in spite of this He loves us and Jesus died for us.

Love getting into orbit

As we saw in an earlier chapter,[1] we love God whom we have not seen by loving those whom we can see (see 1 Jn. 4: 20). Loving God with all our heart, soul, mind and strength does not exclude love for others besides God; rather it insists upon it as a proof of true love for God. To love Him like that is the basis for loving my rather unlikable and unlovely neighbour as myself, as I in turn have been beloved by God in spite of my own lack of comeliness.

Human love is often inhibited at some point in its natural progression. The orphan has no parents to love and looks for others to take their place. Marriage is not the will of God for all, and the love which might have been poured out on husband or wife cannot be used in that way. Paul sees this as setting free the unmarried person for an uninhibited and undivided love for God (1 Cor. 7: 32-34). Instead of serving God by loving one's husband, wife or children, there may be a more direct love for the Lord, to be expressed in love for one's fellowmen more generally. Or again, a married couple may be childless and the expected purpose of marriage may not be fulfilled. This means there will be opportunity to extend the love and money and attention, which might have been poured out upon their own children, to others who are in need of a home, by a welcome to the shy and lonely, the unwanted and the unlovely, or perhaps by formal adoption of those desperately needing a home.

But even supposing there is nothing to inhibit the flowering of married love in the bearing of children, and the love of the family, why should this love stop there and not continue to flow outwards and onwards to others in turn? If love is something which is infinitely extensible without diminishing in quality, its joys are not to be

[1] See pp. 19, 20.

enjoyed in isolated self-indulgence, nor yet to be confined to the marriage partner, nor yet to be lavished upon those in blood-relationship alone. The love of marriage and the family should provide, as it were, a kind of launching-platform, the first- and second-stage rockets which lift our love properly into orbit. Because we enjoy marriage and our family so much, then we are ready to love in ever-widening circles. Each new marriage, each new home, has within it tremendous potential for the blessing and good of those around. Instead of having the sense of being excluded, they are themselves drawn in. Perhaps something of this is suggested by the words of the Lord, that in heaven they 'neither marry nor are given in marriage, but are like angels in heaven' (Mt. 22: 30). Not only, with no death, is there no further need for reproduction, but family joy is shared by all before God.

Love between the sexes

This is obviously the place to begin, for from the love of husband and wife springs the love for the children, and the responsive love of children for their parents; and (to avoid any chicken-egg arguments) this is where the Bible starts, with a single human couple. There is a tremendous potential here for good. Every man and woman has in them this potential for starting a family. Here is the alabaster box waiting to be opened and to pour out its ointment. There is also potential here for evil and sorrow, for it can be spoiled by playing with it and experimenting with it. How often it can be cheapened by experimental adventures: we want to use it now, or at least we want to be sure that everything works all right.

The Japanese have a story about a box which was not to be opened. A fisherman, as a reward for kindness to a turtle, is granted a visit to the Dragon Palace at the bottom of the sea. After being lavishly entertained for a few days he asks to return and is given a box which he is told not to open. When he gets back to his former village he finds that his house has disappeared and all whom he had known have long since died. Feeling desperately alone, he forgets his instructions and opens the box. There is a puff of white smoke, and he is immediately transformed into an extremely old, utterly senile dodderer. One is left with a tremendous sense of existential desolation and estrangement as the old man waits for death on the seashore. His youth has gone irretrievably for ever.

It has nothing directly to do with this story, but there is a sense in which sexual love is a little like a sealed box marked 'not to be opened until your wedding-day'. But in times of isolation and loneliness we are tempted to open the box. Will I please God in the way in which I use this wonderful gift of sexual love? Am I prepared to entrust it to Him until the time of His choosing? The Christian is one who recognizes the will of God as the best for him. He wants the very best for me, and I am ready to trust Him. The law of God is not something repressive or hindering free expression, but 'the precepts of the Lord are right, rejoicing the heart; the commandment of the Lord is pure, enlightening the eyes; the fear of the Lord is clean, enduring for ever' (Ps. 19: 8, 9). There is a health and sanity and spontaneity about the will of God for us, in every respect, including this one.

Premature expression[2]

There are increased physiological pressures. The evidence seems confused, but some people believe that statistics indicate that in Britain at least the onset of menstruation has become significantly earlier on average.[3] At the same

[2] See also 'A Time to Embrace . . .', Essays on the Christian View of Sex, edited by Oliver R. Barclay (IVF, 1964).

[3] See, however, C. G. Scorer, The Bible and Sex Ethics Today (Tyndale Press, 1966), p. 102.

time, the actual age for marriage seems to have become progressively later among better-educated people. In addition to the consequent physiological pressures, there are the psychological pressures resulting from the use of sex by mass media for advertising purposes, and on all sides we are being told of the rapidly collapsing standards of the society around us. We do well to recognize these pressures, while realizing that the situation was not so dissimilar in the pagan world into which the first Christians went with the gospel.

The Bible is utterly realistic and frighteningly relevant to the problem of young people today. It is not in the least 'Victorian' or 'prudish' in its approach to sex. It holds up a frank picture of both the blessings and the tragedy which can result from the proper use or the misuse of sex. There are some stark stories of those who would not wait. The first book of the Bible tells the story of Shechem, the young prince who truly loved young Dinah, but who would not or could not wait to do things the proper way and thus antagonized the girl's family (Gn. 34). It was a case of true love: his soul was drawn to Dinah, he loved the maiden and spoke tenderly to her. Shechem's father and Shechem himself asked for her hand, but her family knew that he had already lain with her and they were 'very angry, . . . for such a thing ought not to be done'. The young man did not delay to accept the condition of circumcision, because 'he had delight in Jacob's daughter', but it was made the opportunity of treacherous murder by the girl's indignant brothers. It was true love, but it went wrong.

Sometimes, of course, it is more lust's counterfeit of love. The story of Amnon and Tamar might once have been considered unfit for public reading (2 Sa. 13). But this sad tale could scarce encourage anyone to sin, so plainly do we read its terrible warning to young people in any generation. Amnon was so tormented over this beautiful girl that he made himself ill. He had fallen in love; or had he? The girl seemed quite unattainable because of their blood affinity. So there was the sorry stratagem to get the girl to his bedroom to nurse him in his sickness. This very lack of honesty and the under-handedness of the whole affair condemn it at once. The girl pleaded with him: 'such a thing is not done' (echo of the Shechem-Dinah story); it is 'wanton folly'. Let him speak to the king, her father; permission perhaps was not impossible, and it seems that if the thing were done properly, she had no objection to him. But he would not listen, and no sooner had he had his way than he hated her 'with very great hatred'.

He told her to get out. She begged to be allowed to stay; to be sent away was a greater wrong. She eventually went away crying and dwelt desolate in her brother's house. The king was angry, but his own recent moral behaviour was also culpable and he did nothing. Again it is the girl's brother who took revenge and killed Amnon.

The lesson of these two sad stories is plain: the love of man and woman is too precious a thing to toy with. In both cases it is the failure to do the proper thing which infuriates those responsible for the girl. We cannot just dismiss this as 'convention'. The convention is for the protection of young women, and for that matter of young men, and for the proper ordering of society. In one place Ezekiel (22: 11) lists various sexual sins with other forms of social injustice. Consent has nothing to do with it. Immorality overthrows the proper ordering of society. It seems inconsistent to be passionate about some social evils, and not to be equally passionate about the wicked-ness of sexual immorality. In the United States now in one year an average of 400,000 couples are divorced and, in consequence, half a million children, two-thirds of them under the age of ten, have their home life dis-rupted; that is, half a million children each year. About half of those who are getting divorces now are themselves the children of divorced parents, so that early insecurity seems to breed insecurity for life. Irresponsible use of the sex instincts can be socially destructive, quite apart from whether it is now possible to prevent conception or not. That another person's emotions should be played upon and then cast rudely aside, leaving them emotionally in turmoil until they enter another relationship which may be as abruptly terminated, means that sex is debased to a merely mechanical function, and destroys the foundation upon which a satisfying and happy marriage can be built.

Responsible courtship

There are two good questions to ask before embarking upon courtship. The word has a pleasant, winsome flavour to it, perhaps because it sounds so like courtesy. However, to be brutally biological, in the animal kingdom courtship is the preliminary to mating. This means that before courting we should ask: Is marriage intended? If it is not, then we are behaving irresponsibly and very uncharitably. We are just trifling with the love that another person has to offer.

'Like a madman who throws firebrands,
    arrows, and death,
  is the man who deceives his neighbour
    and says, "I am only joking!"' (Pr. 26: 18, 19).

But there is a second question; for marriage may be seriously intended, but the person concerned may still be young or facing a course of study which means he may have to remain unmarried for several years. A good second question then is: Is marriage foreseeable? If marriage is not possible in the foreseeable future, then we are unwise to allow friendship to develop into courtship. If the courtship cannot lead to anything for a very long time, then it may be selfish of one and cruel to the other. Driving with the emotional brakes on for years and years can be hard on the emotional linings!

Surely if, in this matter also, our longing is to please God, then we shall want to use our capacity for love in the way which pleases Him most. We shall not be content with a moderately successful performance, but only with excellence.

Failure

To some, that last sentence might be discouraging; we may aim at excellence, but what if we fail? Thus James 3: 2 reads: 'For we all make many mistakes . . .' or, in the older version, 'For in many things we offend all . . .', and whatever our aims and ideals may be, there can be few who have no room for any regrets over failure. Even when mistakes have been made, perhaps we may aim at excellence in the way in which we seek to regain the right road. Even where there has been the most miserable failure, and we feel farthest from excellence, the Lord will meet with us at the point of our deepest need and repentance, and show us how to regain the road.

Sometimes there may be no escaping the consequences of failure. Just as David lived to the end with Bathsheba, and always the remembrance of the brave and scrupulous retainer, whom he had sent to his death to get her, must have been with him, yet she was the mother of the crown prince (2 Sa. 11; 12). The Bible does not shrink from the hard facts of the case. The grace of God is needed, not only at the point of failure, but also in the living on with the results of it. The fact that David was in fact forgiven, and we have Psalms 51 and 32 to show his attitudes at the time, did not mean that he could wash his hands of the whole matter. What he had done, he had done, and he still had to suffer the results of it: the hostility of Ahithophel the counsellor, the girl's grandfather who knew all the facts; the seed of his own bad example on the morals of his own grown sons, Amnon and Absalom. It all makes sad reading. And yet it can still be said of this same man, who unified his country and brought it to the place of its greatest material glory, that he was in God's sight 'a man after my heart, who will do all my will' and one who 'served the counsel of God in his own generation' (Acts 13: 22, 36). The Lord Himself is the Friend of sinners, whom He calls to become saints, and our gospel is good news for sinners.

'There's a way back to God from the dark paths of sin;
 There's a door that is open and you may go in:
At Calvary's cross is where you begin,
 When you come as a sinner to Jesus.'

Christian fidelity

The Christian teaching on marriage as strict monogamy is always being attacked by somebody though usually the self-excusing motives are evident. Thus Shelley wrote:
  'I never was attached to that great sect,
   Whose doctrine is, that each one should select
   Out of the crowd a mistress or a friend,
   And all the rest, though fair and wise, commend
   To cold oblivion . . .'
Shelley's doctrine was obviously quite otherwise—and so it can be asked 'whether in the life of any poet there is such a trail of disasters as that which this "beautiful but ineffectual angel" left behind him from 1811 to 1816, in full conviction of his own righteousness and his importance in the regeneration of the world'.[4] The results of Shelley's approach were seen in desertions, suicides, illegitimate children, jealousy and, in a word, everything as far removed from what is angelic or beautiful as can be

4 G. Sampson, *The Concise Cambridge History of English Literature* (CUP, 1941), p. 633.

imagined. This is, of course, exactly what the Bible warns as the results of infidelity:

'. . . lest you give your honour to others
    and your years to the merciless;
lest strangers take their fill of your wealth,
    and your labours go to the house of an alien;
and at the end of your life you groan,
    when your flesh and body are consumed . . .'

(Pr. 5: 9–11).

The kind of policy advocated by Shelley, and those who have agreed with his view, can lead only to loss of security and happiness for wife and children, to loss of honour and respect for the husband, for wasted years, wasted money and a wasted life. The writer of Proverbs goes on to ask rhetorically: 'Can a man carry fire in his bosom and his clothes not be burned?' It suggests that it is utter folly for all that will commit adultery, for the result will be self-destruction, wounds and dishonour, disgrace and the unappeased anger of the wronged parties (Pr. 6: 23–35).

The Bible makes its point that in fact God's way is the way of blessing and genuine fulfilment, the way of health and the way of joy and peace of mind.

'Drink water from your own cistern,
    flowing water from your own well.
Should your springs be scattered abroad,
    streams of water in the streets?
Let them be for yourself alone,
    and not for strangers with you.
Let your fountain be blessed,
    and rejoice in the wife of your youth,
    a lovely hind, a graceful doe.
Let her affection fill you at all times with delight,
    be infatuated always with her love'

(Pr. 5: 15–19).

There is nothing 'Victorian' or falsely prudish in this Bible teaching. There is to be a very real and deep married love between the partners. The secular view might query the word 'always', feeling that the wine of marriage may get stale and flat with the years. But the Christian view knows that, when Jesus is called to the marriage, though the first wine is very good, contrary to common expectation the wine gets better and better! (Jn. 2: 10).

Poor Shelley seems to have been misled at every point. One can but remark at the extreme self-centredness that suggests that 'cold oblivion' was the fate of any woman who did not have a liaison with him. It illustrates well the basic self-centredness of the anti-Christian view, that in satisfying his personal desire he must deprive or wrong others, he must choose one and leave another with a sense of jealousy and desolation. But he is wrong again, in that, as we have seen, the Christian doctrine is not a selfish doctrine which commends others to cold oblivion. 'Forsaking all other' means surely as a wife, as a marriage partner, and there is no end to the richness of the family life that springs out of that exclusive relationship, and the warmth of the welcome that reaches out from their home to bless others. The happily married Christian couple long that their friends may enjoy the same blessing, not create problems for other people's marriages, as Shelley did!

It is the security of the exclusive relationship, upon which the Bible insists, which is the foundation for the security of the family and the extension of that blessing to an ever-increasing circle.

Well then, will I please God with my sex life and my marriage? 'Do not yield your members to sin as instruments of wickedness, but yield yourselves to God as men who have been brought from death to life, and your members to God as instruments of righteousness' (Rom. 6: 13). As Frances Havergal writes of offering her life, time, money, intellect, heart, will, hands and feet, surely our 'members' include our eyes, our senses, our sex: all these too are to be given to Him as instruments of righteousness. Love is a gift He has given us, a capability which He has given me. May I pour out the love locked in the alabaster box in a gloriously fragrant marriage relationship, pleasing to the Lord, and a blessing to the marriage partner, whom He has chosen for me.

Equal partners

In a letter to the Laodicean church we read of the Lord's loathing of lukewarmness (Rev. 3: 16). But if a keen and active Christian, be he or she ever so warm in the faith (in Japan we call them 'hot-hearted' Christians), marry a cold, unwarmed Christian, then if the two are put together, even if the cold one is a little warmed, the end result is two lukewarm Christians! It is important that we marry one whom we know is as eager to serve Christ as we are ourselves, indeed one whom we respect as being a more mature Christian than ourselves. Self-depreciation means that this respect will be mutual: it is not like telling a learner at tennis to improve his play by always partnering someone better! In fact, of course, one will be more mature than the other, but there will be equality of respect. That is to say, dedication to Christ should be one of the things that we look for in a potential marriage partner, in addition to qualities of physical attractiveness and intellectual compatibility. It is not enough that he or she is a hanger-on at some church, or that they decorate themselves with a badge of some kind. This may mean very little, like the caption in the jeweller's shop over some delicate little silver crosses on slender chains: 'Show your Christianity unobtrusively'! We need to be sure that for the other person their faith is not just something appended to a busy schedule, but that there is wholehearted commitment to the Lord for every part of life.

It is hard to use your home for the Lord if one partner is always hanging back, rather than pressing on and eager to use everything for the Lord. What this book has been saying about the whole-hearted individual is obviously applicable also to the whole-hearted couple, and an unsuitable match can be a tremendous hindrance. It is, unfortunately, not uncommon to find that a committed Christian has married a 'Christian' whose dedication is not the same, and to see their combined faith cool to a tepid tradition of chilly church-going as the years go by. The partner who might have been so effective has been neutralized by a spiritually mediocre partner. On the mission field, even, while some men are kept on the field by the magnificent support of their wives (for it is the woman who keeps the man from cracking), in other cases one sees that a man is not half as useful as he might have been had he married a more devoted woman. In a small group within society, and especially in church youth groups or small Christian Unions, people tend to be attracted to the most attractively eligible person in the same group, and may rush into an alliance which is later regretted, for in a larger context, with more competition, they may not seem so attractive.

Many students regard university as the best marriage market, the largest context, and feel that if they are not successful here, there will be scant choice later on when in the smaller groups of society. But time must always increase the circle of eligible acquaintants, and increasing maturity seems to make us better judges of what we really need in a life partner, even if it gets harder to make up one's mind. 46% of all divorces are of girls who marry in their teens, and conversely 85% of those who marry after twenty-five years of age stay married. It is the very early marriages which tend to break up (though of course not all of them), and generally those who marry later make a more stable marriage.

It is important therefore to avoid rush and to have the very highest expectations both for ourselves and for others. I shall never forget a silver-haired missionary veteran say with great thankfulness and joy: 'I married a woman who was missionary-hearted from the crown of her head to the tips of her toes!' They enjoyed together many years of combined usefulness in the villages of India, and were an example and inspiration to younger generations of students. There need be no fear of missing the best. The Lord is concerned that we have the very best, and there is a great joy in trusting the Lord, for He can be trusted. There is no 'risk' involved in trusting Him for our marriage, to 'arrange' it for us.

The single-minded life

There is an unfortunate tendency to look down on or to imagine that those who remain single, whether from choice or of necessity, have chosen a less worthy path. The Bible, on the contrary, in a number of places (*e.g.* Mt. 19: 12; 1 Cor. 7: 32ff.) makes it clear that such a state has its advantages in keeping a person free for a more single-minded devotion to directly spiritual purposes. Single people have more time for study and for other people than those who must feed, entertain and police their own children. A missionary mother, for example, if she has several children, can be so absorbed in fulfilling her God-given ministry to her own children that she has little time for direct missionary work, and even the father may be restricted in his activity unless the children are well disciplined. Anybody who has tried to study in a room with small children soon realizes the problem. This is not to say that their ministries are inferior or superior; merely that the single person has time for others in a way that the married person often has not.

There is also advantage in remaining single for longer than many contemporaries for the sake of the Christian service that can be done. A married person cannot, and should not, be out night after night, but a single person is able to devote himself much more freely to that kind of voluntary Christian activity in churches, youth clubs and the like. A lot can be said in favour of this kind of deliberate single-mindedness for the kingdom of heaven's sake. For Christians to behave in their early twenties as though getting married was their main aim in life seems a waste of what can otherwise be used purposefully in active Christian service.

Among students there are often strong pressures from non-Christian behaviour around, and even within some Christian Unions, forcing young people to pair off. In view of the limited amount of student time for extra-curricular activities, the Devil must chuckle when time that might otherwise be used for friendships and personal evangelism with fellow-students of the same sex is absorbed in premature billing and cooing. When everybody else is pairing off, it demands great self-control and single-mindedness not to be caught up in the prevailing excitement, *à la* 'Bird Flocks and the Breeding Cycle'. The sight of other individuals of the same species engaging in courtship rituals has a stimulating effect on those individuals not yet paired off.

Certainly the biological urge is strong, and it is further strengthened by seeing others courting. The Christian needs to pray for single-mindedness and the ability to distinguish what is really the Lord's leading from the wish-fulfilling coincidences which are used to excuse conformity to the prevailing pattern of pairing off. Like Samson, a young man's time and energies may be wasted on temporary infatuations, and he may look back and wonder how he did so little in those years of great potential.

Divided loyalty?

'The unmarried man is anxious about the affairs of the Lord, how to please the Lord; but the married man is anxious about worldly affairs, how to please his wife, and his interests are divided. And the unmarried woman or girl is anxious about the affairs of the Lord, how to be holy in body and spirit; but the married woman is anxious about worldly affairs, how to please her husband. I say this for your own benefit, not to lay any restraint upon you, but to promote good order and to secure your undivided devotion to the Lord' (1 Cor. 7: 32–35).

At first sight this suggests a conflict. In some sense there is such a conflict, for although a woman may serve and please God through looking after her husband and children, there is clearly a sense in which she has less time for direct evangelistic activity. However, it is important to remember that this chapter is Paul's answer to a question about the advantages of celibacy, and that it is the advantages that he is dealing with here. It is a valid point, that the unmarried person may love the Lord more directly and without distraction, and can often have a wider circle of activity for Christ. At the same time, as we have seen, there is no conflict for married people in loving the Lord with *all* their heart and in loving their neighbour, wife, husband and children. We do things for them as for the Lord. Through serving them we are able to serve Him.

A glorious example of the balance of Scripture is found in the passage where the Lord Jesus speaks of those whose celibacy may be natural, compelled, or voluntary. These are those eunuchs 'who have made themselves eunuchs for the sake of the *kingdom of heaven*' (Mt. 19: 12). However, lest any should press the Lord's words to an extreme in suggesting that this is of necessity the higher calling, the event which immediately follows is that of the mothers bringing their children for His blessing. That is, these uncelibate women bring their children to Him, and His words are in the context (as always) deeply significant: 'Let the children come to me, and do not hinder them; for to such belongs the *kingdom of heaven*' (Mt. 19: 14). Not only are those to be blessed who have remained unmarried for the sake of the kingdom of heaven, but also blessed are those who through marriage have produced children for that same kingdom of heaven. Both paths are blessed of the Lord.

Thus in Ephesians (6: 2ff.) Paul sees no incongruity in urging husbands to love their wives to the degree to which Christ loved the church and gave Himself for it. This love between married Christians can be a picture of the love of Christ. Then let our love be offered to Him, this love potential of the human heart. 'Lord, take my love and bless it and use it for Your glory and the blessing of many.'

Suggestions for prayer and meditation

Do I have secret reservations about Christian teaching on sex and marriage?

Is the One who made us 'male and female' not to be trusted?

Are we determined to seek the very best, joyous use of our sexual powers?

Am I therefore prepared to wait for His will for my life to be made clear, and not to rush prematurely into relationships without proper consideration?

Do I want to demonstrate, to the pagan world at large, the sanity, beauty and balance of the Christian teaching about sex and marriage?

Have I given these 'members' of mine, including my sex, to the Lord?

Lord, please help me to glorify You in my use of this power to love. If it pleases You to give me a marriage partner, and children, may I excel in loving them for You; and if it is Your will for me to be unmarried, may I accept this joyfully and willingly, and pour out my love for You to give fragrance to all around. In Jesus' name. Amen.

7 SPECTATORS or PLAYERS?

Take my hands, and let them move
At the impulse of Thy love.
Take my feet, and let them be
Swift and beautiful for Thee.

A naval officer friend of mine once told me the story of how, when the whole ship's company were paraded on deck, and all the other watches were performing some duty except his own which was still waiting for orders, there was a shout from the bridge: 'For God's sake, *do* something!' Better let men double up and down than stand there idly doing nothing! And 'for God's sake' we Christians are called to go into action. A Christian is meant to be 'doing something' for his Master.

A book of action

The Bible is the history of God in action among men, God doing things to save men. When God is in action He usually seems to call upon individual men to act with Him and for Him, and for His sake to 'do something'. The Bible seems to be a history of utterly frustrating circumstances, of human failure and helplessness; then God raises up somebody to lead the people out of their desperate situation. When the Israelites are slaves in Egypt, building great cities for the Pharaoh, God raises up Moses to go and tell Pharaoh: 'Let my people go!' When Moses dies, Joshua, another man of action, is ready to take his place, trained up to be his successor. In the period which follows, Israel over and over again is conquered by some alien people (often permitted as a punishment for unfaithfulness to the One True God), and God raises up a succession of men (and women, like Deborah): first the judges, Othniel, Ehud, Shamgar, Barak, Gideon, Jephthah, Samson, Samuel, and the kings, Saul and David, and later the prophets, Elijah and Elisha, Isaiah, Jeremiah and Ezekiel. Finally the state of Israel is such that through Ezekiel (22: 30) God says: 'I sought for a man among them who should build up the wall and stand in the breach before me for the land, that I should not destroy it; but I found none.'

Earlier there had been the kings, Josiah and Hezekiah, who had called their people back to repentance and a pure worship of the Lord; but now there was nobody. The whole Old Testament account seems to be one of God looking for men who are prepared to give themselves unreservedly to Him for His service.

The man of action

The Lord Jesus Himself, who went around 'doing good' (Acts 10: 38), was supremely the man of action, the man who stood in the breach, who knew that what God wanted was not animal sacrifice, but One who would give the 'body' prepared for Him, 'to do thy will, O God' (Heb. 10: 5–7). This man, who came to finish the work which His Father had given Him to do, and who finished that work on the cross, was also the One who taught His disciples the need for action.

Is this not the point of many of the parables? In the parables of the talents and the pounds, which we have already considered,[1] it is the man who *did nothing* who is condemned. It is the man who failed to act when he

[1] See pp. 39ff., 49ff.

might have acted. In the parable of the sheep and the goats, the terrible indictment is reserved for those who did nothing in the face of human need and suffering: 'Depart from me, you cursed, into the eternal fire prepared for the devil and his angels; for I was hungry and you gave me no food, I was thirsty and you gave me no drink, I was a stranger and you did not welcome me, naked and you did not clothe me, sick and in prison and you did not visit me' (Mt. 25: 41–43). I was hungry and what did you do? Nothing. I was in prison and what did you do? Nothing. I was naked and what did you do? Nothing.

The final great command of Christ is a command to go and do something. 'Go therefore and make disciples of all nations, baptizing them . . . teaching them to observe all that I have commanded you' (Mt. 28: 19, 20). Go and *do* something: make disciples, and teach those disciples to go and *do* all that I have commanded you to *do*, including, of course, making more disciples and teaching them to go and *do* . . . In modern terminology it was a command to 'get cracking'. The men of the New Testament, no less than the men of the Old, are called to be men of action: it is not surprising, then, that the next book of the New Testament should be called the *Acts* of the Apostles. These were men sent out by the Lord Jesus, to act for Him in the power of His Spirit.

The God of action

This emphasis is not surprising, because the God of the Bible is a God who acts, who does things. This idea is in marked contrast to the currently popular 'ground of our being' kind of God who operates sporadically and rather ineffectually in some deep substratum of human consciousness. He seems to be thought of as a kind of 'cosmic tapioca pudding',[2] an inoffensive and elusively self-effacing 'being' who seems reluctant to interfere decisively in human affairs, acting only indirectly through agents, if at all, and even that is open to doubt! All offensive, biblical, primitive anthropomorphism must be removed! Actually all that is being done is to substitute another terminology—using images of space and depth—for the biblical terminology which uses images of personality and height.

The God of the Bible, however, is a God who does things, a God of action. He speaks, He creates, He acts, He intervenes, He shakes the nations, He touches the mountains and they smoke, He makes the hills skip like rams and the little hills like lambs, He rules with a rod of iron, His pathway is in the whirlwind and in the storm and the clouds are the dust of His feet. He is a great King. It is all extremely and offensively anthropomorphic, but it does convey very clearly the fact that God is gloriously alive and triumphantly in action. He acts powerfully and appropriately, graciously and irresistibly, in justice and in judgment. Who was ever afraid of a 'ground of being', this amorphous, jelly-like, ectoplasmic spirit? But when men encounter the God of the Bible they fall on their faces (thus Daniel, Ezekiel, John) and have always to be reassured, 'Fear not . . .' Fear and awe are the automatic reactions of men when they meet God. All the superlatives that Paul can muster cannot adequately express the might and the strength and the power and the dynamic force of Almighty God.

To meet this God of action is to be immediately challenged to act, to move, to get cracking. We fall down before Him and we say: 'Lord, take my hands, . . . take my feet, . . . Let me be used to serve You.'

[2] C. S. Lewis, *Miracles* (Bles, 1947), p. 78.

Actions to initiate actions

God's men start things. The Philistines had a huge army and an effective arms embargo through a monopoly of iron. They had garrisons at selected points, so that Israel was an occupied country under surveillance from military strongholds. Then Jonathan attacked one of these strongholds, accompanied only by his armour-bearer, and, by a process of escalation, this attack led to the rout of all the occupying forces. Jonathan's action was a very brave action, only on a very small scale. He killed twenty men in about half an acre of ground. It was little more than a minor skirmish. But this one bold deed set the ball rolling, and initiated an action that led to a great victory.

When the Philistines returned again in force, they brought with them a secret weapon in the form of a great bragging oaf called Goliath. The Israelite warriors sat on the other side of the valley for forty days, goggling at this behemoth and shaking in their shoes. Then God's man of action arrives, totally unequipped with weapons, and inexperienced, but incensed that there should be such an affront to God. He takes on the giant and, to everybody's astonishment, slays him. He slew only one man, but this began the action and the whole Philistine force was routed.

Both Jonathan and David initiated action on a small front, just where they were, but what they did led to great victories. There is a need for us also to take the field locally. We cannot hope to take on the whole of the enemy force, but we do not have to do so. 'There's a work for Jesus ready at your hand,' as the hymn says, and we are called to be bold and to take the initiative where we are. God will take care of the rest when, as a result of our action, the battle spreads along the whole front.

Two men are being burnt at the stake in what is now Broad Street, Oxford. They must have been only too conscious of their own great weakness and insignificance in the face of their enemies. But, says Latimer, 'Be of good cheer, Master Ridley, . . . we shall this day, by God's grace, light such a torch in England as (I trust) will never be put out . . .' and though many attempts have been made to snuff that Protestant candle in the English church, it still burns today.

It may be Luther nailing his theses to a door in Wittenberg, it may be Raikes starting the first Sunday school, William Booth setting out to preach in the slums, Hudson Taylor praying on the beach at Brighton, Josiah Spiers tracing out a text for the children on the beach at Llandudno . . . all these Christian men were men of action, whose initiative, in trembling dependence upon God, led others out into effective service for Christ. They started something and the Lord blessed them and gave great victories.

We need that same desire to start something today, whether in starting a witnessing group in a factory, inviting neighbourhood wives in for coffee and Bible study, a discussion in the office, a young people's Bible club or children's Sunday school. It may be a Scripture Union branch or an evangelical library. It was an American girl of sixteen who started a Scripture Union movement for adults in Japan, at a time when membership in other countries, including Britain, was still mainly for children. One Japanese schoolmaster has already started three churches, by gathering a little group to study the Bible and continuing on until there was a group of converted families and they were able to call a pastor. Shall we give our hands and feet to the Lord to become those who initiate some work for Him in *our* district?

Actions to right wrongs

When Nahash the Ammonite threatened to humiliate the men of Jabesh, and they sent messengers to Saul, he was filled with indignation, the Holy Spirit came mightily upon him, and Israel rallied to him as one man. He promised relief before the sun was up, and that meant a night march along the Arabah, the great volcanic rift-valley through which the Jordan runs. It was a man of action who rallied his people to right a great wrong.

The prophets' proclamation of judgment was often on account of civil wrongs. Nathan confronted David about his crime against Uriah, Elijah confronted Ahab when he went to take possession of the vineyard of Naboth, and John the Baptist fearlessly challenged Herod for his immoral life. When the Roman law had been broken in Philippi, Paul insisted that the offenders apologized and refused to leave until they did so (Acts 16: 37ff.). Our evangelical forefathers in Britain, Wilberforce and Shaftesbury, were men who took a strong stand politically against the social evils of the day, and were able to overcome the entrenched forces of self-interest. It is regrettable that suspicion of those who had a 'social gospel', but no saving gospel, has meant that Evangelicals of our own day have tended to be silent on social issues. It is questionable whether resolutions by church bodies are either necessary or effective, but at the very least there is a field of action here for Christian individuals, whose calling is to make a clear Christian stand in the political realm.

In a one-party state there is a real dilemma when a government has apparently lost its mandate to govern, and is no longer fulfilling the divinely ordained functions of government. How right, then, is the Christian to seek to overthrow such a government, and by what means? This was the dilemma of German Christians when it was clear that Nazism was not an acceptable form of government. The Jews who were descendants of the revolutionary Maccabees presumably found no more difficulty in justifying such action than do North Americans their rebellion in 1775! Fortunately in a democracy there are perfectly legal means of overthrowing governments which no longer have a mandate to govern. The Christian who is concerned for social justice will have to act politically in order to right wrongs.

All over the world among young people there seems to be a rising tide of concern for social justice. An American Inter-Varsity Christian Fellowship worker recently related [3] an experience at a meeting where he was quizzed, 'What have you personally done to help bring about social justice in our day?' They were concerned to know that what he was saying to them was not just so many words, not claiming to be committed when that commitment had never been consummated in action. They had no time for a phoney; the concern expressed for his fellow men must be shown to be a genuine one.

The same magazine contained some interesting comments from a Christian who had been taking part in some of the student demonstrations. 'Christianity seemed very drab and dull after Free Speech Movement rallies and picketing. Christian idealism about Someone who lived two thousand years ago seemed irrelevant compared to the real world of students, who really cared about freedom to learn truth and to act on that truth. Church people seemed stodgy and conservative compared to student demonstrators.' While we may question whether the atmosphere of a demonstration is quite what one would regard as desirable for a Christian meeting, this quotation does seem to suggest that we have lost, or failed to pass on, the revolutionary spirit of the Acts of the Apostles, or the Reformation, or during the repression of the Puritan nonconformists by the state church in England 1660–1668, or during the Evangelical Revival. It is staid and respectable to be a Christian at this particular juncture in history, and nobody seems very eager for it to be otherwise.

When the church takes on a spectator role rather than an active role, when it stops being the church militant and becomes the church quiescent, no wonder it seems

[3] *His* magazine, June 1964.

dull. It *is* dull. It needs revival and a return to the Word of God, that its conscience may be quickened and that holy indignation may burn. So often the church seems to be on the side of the *status quo* and the conservative establishment, right or wrong. There is no need to alter or modify the biblical message to meet modern circumstances; all we need to do is to return to the essential biblical content of that message.

Actions to overcome hatred and misunderstanding

Much secular action involves working up hatred of the 'other side'. Orwell's 1984 'hate sessions' remind one very much of 'confrontation' and the deliberate working up of national or class hatred that seem so much part of the political method of the twentieth century. Bitterness and resentment is built up between the two sides; each has a chip on his shoulder. Injustice and unfair treatment is expected; a suspicious, critical attitude is met with corresponding suspicion. Like David in the affair of churlish Nabal (1 Sa. 25), he has his sword girded on his thigh and he means to use it. Nabal had insulted them, and was ungrateful for all the help he had received. But the intelligent and beautiful Abigail had the sense to realize the folly of what her husband had done, and her prompt act of conciliation, apology and explanation not only saved the lives of her husband and her household, but kept David back from taking vengeance into his own hands and sullying his own name.

In the following chapter Saul has come with three thousand men to capture David. David, great guerilla leader that he is, with Abishai in support, infiltrates the camp and gets right up to the sleeping Saul. He makes off with Saul's spear and water-jar, but leaves him unharmed, much to the disgust of Abishai, who regarded it as a providential opportunity to remove Saul from the scene for ever. What was David's purpose in drawing attention to their successful and peaceful raid? Was it just to gibe at Abner for not keeping better watch? The result was that Saul was smitten in conscience: he should have been dead, but had been spared through the kindness of the man whom he had been hounding for months and seeking to kill. By this definite act of mercy to his enemy, David made it hard for Saul to go on hating him. By returning good for evil, David cooled the hatred of Saul; in a deeper sense of the word, than by merely removing his spear, he 'disarmed' him.

'Beloved, never avenge yourselves, but leave it to the wrath of God; for it is written, "Vengeance is mine. I will repay, says the Lord." No, "if your enemy is hungry, feed him; if he is thirsty, give him drink . . ." Do not be overcome by evil, but overcome evil with good' (Rom. 12: 19–21). In other words, as Christians we should make a definite point of discovering what are the needs of the man who dislikes us and, by seeking to do him a service, we should show love for him and destroy the hostility. The Christian is to be a 'man of action' in this sense also, not in seeking to destroy his enemy, but to destroy the enmity, by taking positive steps to make contact with him and to do something for him.

'Love your enemies and pray for those who persecute you . . .' (Mt. 5: 44). 'Blessed are the peacemakers, for they shall be called sons of God' (Mt. 5: 9). Here is a definite sphere of Christian action, to seek to break down the hatred which others may bear by positively seeking to show friendship and kindness.

Actions to counteract failures

Israel has crossed the Jordan, advanced into Canaanite territory and captured the walled city of Jericho. Now they have been defeated and have fled before the men of insignificant Ai, and the people are in terror. Joshua begins to pray, but God asks him what he is praying for. Get up, go and do something. Go and put right the sin which has been committed (Jos. 7). There are times when what is called for is not prayer, but action. The error had to be put right before there could be any expectation of victory. It was a time for practical repentance. Prayer is not a substitute for action. Prayer is not meant to accompany inaction, but to be the guide and support of action.

Elijah had won a terrific victory over the prophets of Baal and the power of God had been demonstrated in the sight of all. The long struggle was over, it seemed. Then comes the realization that Jezebel is still very much alive and thirsting for his blood (1 Ki. 19). Elijah flees for his life, and finally, physically and emotionally exhausted, he prays for death. He wants to give up; there seems to be no end to the conflict and battle, and he just feels that he cannot go on any longer. The angel of God sees that he is rested and fed, essential parts of the cure of his depression. Then comes the word of the Lord to him, 'What are you doing here, Elijah?' And Elijah is reassured of eventual victory, and sent back to anoint three men who will be the scourge of Baal worship: a new king for Syria, a new king for Samaria, and Elisha to be his own successor. But it was not only the appointment of successors to carry on the struggle. Elijah himself still has important tasks to perform, especially in the famous confrontation with Ahab in the vineyard of Naboth, wickedly slain, when Elijah prophesies the death of Ahab and the destruction of his house, and the terrible end of Jezebel herself (1 Ki. 21). He also prophesies the death of Ahab's successor Ahaziah, because he inquired of false gods instead of asking the Lord (2 Ki. 1). Elijah thought he had failed and was finished, yet the Lord recommissioned him and sent him out again to act, and so laid the foundation for the final overthrow of the tyrants.

Peter too had failed, but at that quiet breakfast gathering by the shore of the lake, the man who had three times denied his Lord, three times declared his love and was commissioned to go out into action, to feed Christ's lambs and sheep (Jn. 21).

Even where there has been failure of action, the Christian is called to go back into the fray, to do great exploits for the Lord his God.

Reticence to act

There are, of course, times when it is good to be cautious and to avoid rash and precipitate action. But there is also a danger sometimes that we do nothing in the belief that this is spiritual: we are waiting for God to act. We are leaving it to Him! We have already seen that, in the matter of taking vengeance, we do leave that to God, although we ourselves have been commanded to take definite steps in order to show love to the enemy. God has already given us standing orders on certain matters. We do not need to wait for fresh instructions to feed our enemies, to pray for those that despitefully use us, and so forth. We do not need some special vision before we go out to make disciples, to baptize and teach. It has been laid down that this is our responsibility 'even to the end of the age'. We do not need fresh orders before we do good to all men, especially to those of the household of faith. There can be a false 'quietism', which is really a form of disobedience. 'I was waiting to be told' is not spiritual when we have already been told quite clearly in the Bible what we ought to do.

It is only when the matter is not clear that we need to wait on God to make His will known. 'Leaving it to the Lord' can be camouflage for sloth and cowardice. Our general responsibility is clear without further instructions. In the army, not having read standing orders is no excuse; one is expected to know and ignorance is no plea. The Bible commands action and we do well to be sure that we not only know what the Lord has commanded, but also that we seek to obey that which we know.

But there are other instances in which there are matters of more individual responsibility. The Bible shows men as often being extremely reticent to act and to take up work for God. An interesting example is that of Samuel (1 Sa. 16), after Saul has failed. The one man who could now act is reluctant to do so. We can understand his reluctance, for four reasons: (1) he had opposed having a king in the first place; (2) the man that he had anointed had failed; (3) perhaps the next man would fail as well; and (4) in any case to make any move to anoint a successor would be an extremely hazardous proceeding. It was probable that Saul was having him watched in case he made any such move, for Samuel had already said that the Lord had torn the kingdom from Saul and given it to a neighbour who was better than he. It was clearly much the most sensible thing to sit tight and watch events. Let us see what God will do. Samuel was the obvious man to act; he had a major responsibility for Saul and the choice of Saul, and for his failure. Who else could really appoint a successor? Then comes the word of the Lord: 'How long will you grieve for Saul?' Up, and be doing, take a horn of oil and go. Samuel protests the danger, but his responsibility is plain: this is a job for Samuel which no other person really can do.

Moses put up excuse after excuse to avoid the clear commission which the Lord was giving him (Ex. 3 and 4). 'Who am I to go to Pharaoh . . .?' 'I am not sure how to explain about You to Israel . . .' 'They will not believe me . . .' 'I am not eloquent . . .' and finally, 'Oh, my Lord, send, I pray, some other person.' It is not surprising that we read that the anger of the Lord was kindled against Moses, for here was a man who was calling God 'My Lord' and refusing to obey. He had the promise of God's presence and help, and still he was making excuses not to go and do.

Men are reluctant to act. They may even demand remarkable signs in evidence that God has called them. Thus Gideon is commanded, 'Go in this might of yours and deliver Israel from the hand of Midian' (Jdg. 6: 14). He pleads the insignificance of his family, and his own insignificance. He asks for a sign and is given it, and he knows that this is of God. He makes his first trembling step of obedience and destroys the family altar for Baal worship. Then he asks for another sign, and then for another. We too are called to act, but all of us would rather leave it to somebody else. 'Send some other person.' The Bible is a call to action, to present our hands and feet to Him for His service.

> 'His Hands and Feet and Heart, all three,
> Were pierced for me on Calvary,
> And here and now, to Him I bring
> My hands, feet, heart, an offering.'

Suggestions for prayer and meditation

Am I content to be a passive spectator type of Christian?

What initiative have I taken to start some work for Christ?

Am I waiting for more guidance when the instructions have already been given?

Just what am I actually doing for the Lord? Is there no more that I can do?

Are there any people who I know dislike me? Is there anything I can do for them?

Have I given up trying because I have failed at something I have attempted?

Why not make a list of possible things that I might be able to do for Christ—in my neighbourhood? at my work? in my church? in my family? Then make these things a regular matter for prayer and ask for opportunities of seeing them realized.

Are there sick to be visited? Old, lonely people? A local prison or remand home? Is there somewhere that a Christian bookstall could be started? A Scripture Union group? A Bible class? Could my home be used in some way? For soldiers, students or nurses living far away from home? Are there any in this area who seem especially unwelcome or unpopular? Have I any skills which can be used for Christ? Is the local minister expected to visit all the non-Christian homes in the area by himself? How long will it take him if he has no fellow workers who are willing to undertake such a ministry?

There really are plenty of things for which hands and feet are needed. Let me give mine afresh to my Lord.

'Mine are the hands to do the work;
My feet shall run for Thee;
My lips shall sound the glorious news:
Lord, here am I, send me . . .'

HOWARD GUINNESS

8 TALK
or COMMUNICATION?

Take my voice, and let me sing
Always, only, for my King.
Take my lips, and let them be
Filled with messages from Thee.

One of the moving aspects of any consideration of the life of Helen Keller is the fresh realization of the blessing and privilege it is to be able to communicate with other people. To be unable to speak, to be unable to hear, to be unable to understand what others are trying to say, and to be unable to get one's own feelings across must be a terrible experience. A little of the isolation of it can be understood if we ever have to spend a prolonged period alone in a country where nobody speaks English, and where the native language is unknown to us. The sense of alienation and frustration can result in psychological breakdown if it is unduly prolonged, and solitary confinement is used as a means of punishment, even of torture.

Unfortunately we rarely think of this being able to communicate with others as a remarkable and wonderful privilege, except when it is forced upon us by meeting somebody who is deprived of the faculty of communication. We take it for granted and forget the wonder of it. 'I wasn't thinking, just talking,' as a loquacious lady of our acquaintance once remarked. The Venusian Eve encountered by C. S. Lewis's Dr Ransom remarks, 'How often the people of your race speak.' And then she explains, 'You had nothing to say about it and yet made the nothing up into words.' [1]

[1] C. S. Lewis, *Perelandra* (Lane, 1943), p. 61.

It is also sadly true that we can talk to people without ever meaningfully communicating with them. We can confine our remarks to essential business: we want them to give us something ('Please pass the salt') or we exchange information which we both already possess ('Isn't it lovely weather today?'). The faculty of speech need not really exist for such purposes. A man and woman may live as husband and wife in the same house, exchanging a grunt or two from behind the morning paper, between mouthfuls of breakfast, and then a few weary words about the day's doings when the man returns home from work or during the commercials on television, without ever really speaking to each other about what matters most, about what has occupied their deepest thoughts and concerns (most people have some, surely?). The lower animals have various fascinating methods of communicating information, often highly complex, as recent research on bees has shown. Birds communicate by signals and stereotyped sounds indicating warning, courtship, threat, pleasure at laying an egg, and so on. It seems tragic if human beings cannot express things much beyond the state of the weather and their stomachs! This is certainly something which should concern the Christian. Just how useful to God and to His purposes are the words which come out of my mouth each day? If they are not useful, then I might as well be dumb!

A voice vote

'All those in favour, say Aye' may produce the feeblest of responses. Our use of our voices may be a little like our use of the vote. We may use our voices on behalf of God or against Him, or we may just not use our vote at all. Even among professing Christians one gets the impression that the size of the ballot is pretty small sometimes, and that many of those you would expect to come out in support of God's government of the world, just fail to register their conviction. They seem almost indifferent to the outcome of the election; they just cannot be bothered.

Some of us have our mouths open a good deal, not only to put food into them, but to let words come out. But just how far has that advanced the kingdom of God today? Although we claim to believe certain truths, our actual behaviour often seems to belie it. If we really believe what we say we believe, should we not shout it from the housetops and whenever we can get a hearing for it? Perhaps we have decided to leave the matter in the hands of the religious professionals. But apart from their official pulpit utterances, ministers 'off duty' can seem as mundane as everyone else. A recent book on the laity describes them as 'God's Frozen People',[2] and even if the heartsprings are warm enough, it would still be true that many are frozen at the mouth. Is this why the churches are static rather than dynamic? Just frozen stiff. Is this why churches are so often empty, and why it seems increasingly difficult to find Christians apart from on Sundays? Is there some conspiracy of good-mannered silence afoot?

'An important contributory factor to the loss of mental morale by the Church has been a misguided conception of Christian charity. It has been assumed that the charitable man suppresses his views in the same way that he subordinates personal interest. A wild fantasy has taken hold of many Christians. They have come to imagine that just as the unselfish man restrains himself from snatching another piece of cake, so too he restrains himself from putting forward his point of view. And just as it is bad form to boast about your private possessions or loudly recapitulate your personal achievements, so too it is bad form to announce what your convictions are . . .

[2] M. Gibbs and T. R. Morton, *God's Frozen People* (Fontana, 1964).

Of course the very fact that nowadays we look upon convictions as personal possessions is a symptom of the disappearance of the Christian mind. It is precisely in such odd and scarcely graspable notions that the full extent of the secularization of the modern mind is glimpsed.' [3]

It is a most extraordinary distortion of the idea of unselfishness to apply it to the idea that one does not speak about the truth because one happens to believe it for oneself! Just imagine Paul deferring quietly to the Athenians because, after all, they are a philosophical lot of old idolaters, and surrounded by all these old temples deep with cultural significance it would be most tactless to express any Christian convictions. Imagine Peter keeping silent because, after all, one must respect the religious convictions of the Jews, even if one does not agree with them. Imagine John silent among the Gnostics because these things are only a matter of theology in any case, and rather difficult to define.

Good manners may be a cover for shyness—or cowardice. There may be a genuine fear of going in too fast and putting people off. It is the old 'fanatic' phobia again. Anything rather than see that slightly amused, tolerant smile on the faces of those well-mannered people charitably covering up your social gaffe: 'Poor chap's a kind of religious enthusiast. Almost a fanatic!' Caution may be a cover for cowardice.

'Honest to God' and all that

There may, of course, be a fear of merely churning out jargon rather glibly, when it does not really mean anything to the people who hear it. Words like 'salvation' and being 'born again' may be a kind of theological shorthand, but they tend to embarrass other people rather than communicate to them a living experience. There is obvi-

[3] H. Blamires, *The Christian Mind* (SPCK, 1963), pp. 39, 40.

ously some truth in this. But there is also the idea that we must find some fresh way of expressing the old, old story in some way which is acceptable to the modern man; and nobody seems to have been able to do much about it yet. The thing is *sub judice* and various among our 'best theological minds' are looking into the matter, and until they come up with something that really goes across then perhaps we had better keep our mouths shut. There is a commonly accepted idea that the reason for the failure of the churches is the image of God which they have presented to the outside world. The real trouble is that they have not presented any image at all! The gospel has been locked up in a building and not always presented for public inspection even there.

Certainly we must do our utmost to see that the unchanging content of the gospel is presented to the secular society around us in terms which they can understand. But is this really so very difficult? All of us who have been converted from the secular milieu have had to make the effort of understanding the Christian gospel and we have been grasped by it. For when Christian men and women try to explain the significance of their faith to others, they very soon discover what ways of presenting it make sense, and strike a chord, and illuminate the truth, and what do not. Oh, it may not be a very fluent presentation, but the sincerity that goes with it makes up for deficiencies in verbal images. The real trouble about the presentation of the gospel to the secular world has not been so much the way in which it has been presented, but the fact that it often has not been presented at all in any form whatsoever!

The danger of reinterpretation is that what comes out is no longer the gospel. Dr Eric Mascall expresses this rather nicely when discussing Dr Lampe's contribution to *Soundings*, where he offered some reinterpretation of the atonement: 'He (Dr Lampe) has entirely neglected to consider the necessarily analogical nature of all concepts

143

and images that are applied from ordinary human experience to the mysteries of the Christian religion, even those which he himself favours, and that he has therefore been led to reject as unacceptable a great deal of the classical theology of Christendom and set in the place of its rich complexity an over-simplified and impoverished account of his own.' [4]

One would deduce from this that it is better to stick to the Bible and carefully explain its meaning as you go along. But most of all we must be prepared to speak out and tell others about the Lord Jesus, who He is and what He has done and is willing to do for them. Only a congenital idiot would really consider his inability to discover God with the aid of a telescope an insuperable obstacle to faith. What would he expect that kind of 'God' to look like, anyway? Let not moderation close our mouths; though it is to be feared that even preaching to others in moderation might be thought by some to be fanatical! Let us give our mouths to God and use them to tell out His greatness and His grace.

Empty hearts . . . . . empty mouths

There is, however, a more fundamental reason why we may remain silent. The Lord said, 'The good man out of the good treasure of his heart produces good, and the evil man out of his evil treasure produces evil; for out of the abundance of the heart his mouth speaks' (Lk. 6: 45). The New English Bible says, 'The words that the mouth utters come from the overflowing of the heart.' The Lord Jesus Himself so spoke that they all wondered at the gracious words which came out of His mouth; but how we speak depends upon whether our hearts are full of good treasure like His or not. If the heart is poor and impoverished and the treasury is empty, or nearly so,

[4] E. L. Mascall, *Up and Down in Adria* (Faith Press, 1963), p. 83.

small wonder if there is no corresponding richness to be drawn from it. We find that we cannot speak or we do not speak, because we do not feel moved to speak, or we never get round to it, because somehow what we do say sounds stilted, unreal and unsatisfactory. Our experience of Christ may be so faint and so far from reality that we have little to say about it. Because the heart is empty, or nearly so, the mouth is empty as well.

One answer to this is the Morning Watch, the daily Quiet Time: not merely whether we observe a time of prayer and Bible reading as a daily rule of life, but whether we really meet with the Lord or not. Is it a time when we really sit at His feet and listen to His word, really enter into the 'secret place of the Most High'—or just simply a good habit and nothing more? It is not merely a matter of storing Bible verses in one's memory, but of finding that they can be applied in daily experience and the Lord's promises are faithful and effective. Today, the Lord has done this for me, as He said He would. It is here, if we are prepared to be honest, that many of us are so weak. Our testimony is so rarely 'up to the minute' and often dry and dull. What we have to say may be merely an oft-repeated catechism of how we first heard about Christ and were converted umpteen years ago. This account may have lost its freshness through repetition, though it need not. The African brethren in the East African revival area rightly stress the need for fresh testimony. 'We do not want to hear what the Lord has done for you ten years ago. Has He done nothing since then? What has He done for you this week or today that you can tell us about and warm our hearts?' There needs to be this freshness of confession of the heart, that comes from someone who is pressing on day by day, more and more eagerly enjoying life with Christ.

It is this kind of testimony which is bound to carry conviction to the unbelieving sceptic. After all, much of the discussion about images of God almost presupposes an unknown and unexperienced God, and breathes a very different atmosphere from the passionate experience of the Christians of the New Testament. If what comes out of our mouths is an expression of the heart within, then what fails to come out indicates a corresponding lack inside, perhaps even the absence of a genuine faith.

Cleansing

It may not of course be that, but it may be unforgiven sin. A sense of burden and of uncleanness often means that we fear to open our mouths lest we be hypocritical. When Isaiah sees the glory of the Lord in the temple, high and lifted up, he knows that he is undone. 'Woe is me! For I am lost; for I am a man of unclean lips, and I dwell in the midst of a people of unclean lips; for my eyes have seen the King, the Lord of hosts!' (Is. 6: 5). In the presence of God he has this deep sense of the defilement of his mouth. How utterly unsatisfactory and inadequate have been his words, how unclean they have been! Then one of the seraphim flies to him with the burning coal taken from the charred remains of the sacrificed lamb, and with it touches his lips and says, 'Behold, this has touched your lips; your guilt is taken away, and your sin forgiven.' And when this man's mouth has been cleansed he is able to hear God calling for some to go, and he volunteers and the word for him is 'Go, and say to this people . . .' The cleansed mouth is to be used to carry the message of God. What wonderful messages were to come to men through the mouth of Isaiah!

Those of us familiar with the Church of England Prayer Book know well the words: 'O Lord, open thou my lips, and my mouth shall show forth thy praise' (Ps. 51: 15). The context of this verse is extremely significant, set in David's psalm of penitence. Sin has stopped his mouth and taken away his joy in salvation. His lips are locked and his praises are prevented. They cannot praise God without hypocrisy until his sin is forgiven. Not until God has cleansed and purged him, washed him and given him a clean heart, can there be any overflow of spontaneous praise. Not till then can his tongue sing aloud of God's deliverance (Ps. 51: 14). But it seems plain from these verses that it is sin which can stop the mouth, and it is cleansing which will open it.

It is the Christian man, who has been delivered from the horrible pit and the miry clay, whose feet have been set upon a rock, and whose steps have been secured, who can say that God has put in his mouth a new song of praise to God (Ps. 40: 1–3).

Praise

The newly opened mouth will first be occupied in speaking with God, and especially in praise. It is not that the Lord is like some petty-minded person who is always wanting to hear compliments about himself. C. S. Lewis [5] expresses it very well when he says, 'All enjoyment spontaneously overflows into praise . . . The world rings with praise—lovers praising their mistresses, readers their favourite poets, walkers praising the countryside . . .' and he goes on to talk of all the praise you hear of things. He points out that it is the crabbed, malcontent minds which praise least, and the largest minds which find most to praise. He goes on, 'Just as men spontaneously praise whatever they value, so they spontaneously urge us to join them in praising it: "Isn't she lovely? Wasn't it glorious? Don't you think that magnificent?" The Psalmists in telling everyone to praise God are doing what all men do when they speak of what they care about. . . . I think we delight to praise what we enjoy because the praise not merely expresses but completes the enjoyment;

[5] *Reflections on the Psalms* (Bles, 1958), p. 80.

it is its appointed consummation.' Praise is the inevitable result of realizing what kind of Person God is. When the child volunteers 'It is fun going out with you, Daddy', there is this spontaneity of enjoyment, and a desire that the other should share in the joy of it also. It is this exuberant bubbling over of joy in God which is praise.

To the children in the temple the full wonder of the Saviour and His power made them sing out 'Hosanna', and when some could only criticize, the Lord replied to them, 'Have you never read, "Out of the mouth of babes and sucklings thou hast brought perfect praise"?' (Mt. 21: 16, quoting Ps. 8: 2). Again, approaching the city the whole multitude of the disciples began to rejoice and praise God with a loud voice for all the mighty works that they had seen, saying, 'Blessed be the King who comes in the name of the Lord! Peace in heaven and glory in the highest!' And when some of the Pharisees urge Jesus to silence them, He replies, 'I tell you, if these were silent, the very stones would cry out' (Lk. 19: 37–40).

Praise is the product of personal experience of the greatness and glory of God. It is because the heart is full of joy at who He is and what He does, that this overflows through the mouth. There is the desire to express what is in the heart: I must express something of all this that fills my heart with happiness and my eyes with tears. It is the redeemed of the Lord who are pictured in Psalm 126, overwhelmed with God's acts, saying,

"Then our mouth was filled with laughter,
    and our tongue with shouts of joy;
  then they said among the nations,
    "The Lord has done great things for them."
  The Lord has done great things for us; we are glad.'

When a man or woman comes to Jesus Christ, then their mouth seeks to express something of the joy of belonging to Him and they begin to praise God. Thus did the shepherds when they first saw the Christ child (Lk. 2:

20); so were the disciples when the Lord Jesus had ascended (Lk. 24: 53); so were all the first converts following their baptism on the day of Pentecost (Acts 2: 47); and so was the man who had been lame, and who now 'entered the temple with them, walking and leaping and praising God' (Acts 3: 8). This is marvellous, and he had to jump to show what he could do, and his body and his mouth together were just expressing all they could of thankfulness. The warmth of praise often wonderfully unstops and unfreezes the mouth.

It is interesting to see how one thing leads to another, as in Psalm 34:

'I will bless the Lord at all times;
    his praise shall continually be in my mouth' (verse 1).

But it is not enough to rejoice by himself; he must get others to join with him, so he cries,

'O magnify the Lord with me,
    and let us exalt his name together!' (verse 3).

But then there are other people who do not seem to be able to do this. Presumably this is because they have not the same personal experience of this God who saves, so he invites them,

'O taste and see that the Lord is good!
    Happy is the man who takes refuge in him!' (verse 8).

He wants to share this with the youngsters as well,

'Come, O sons, listen to me,
    I will teach you the fear of the Lord' (verse 11),

and then he goes on to instruct them about the proper use of the tongue in words which the apostle Peter later borrowed for the same purpose (1 Pet. 3: 10–12). That is to say, all the uses of the tongue seem to spring forth from its first unloosing. The living water wells up and rushes forth as praise and then is channelled also into other paths of service for the Lord. If we want to use our mouths for God in a way which is pleasing to Him, then praise is the place to begin.

Preaching

There may be preachers who use the so-called 'wordless book',[6] but there can be no 'wordless Christian'. It is impossible to be a silent Christian in a full sense, 'because, if you confess with your lips that Jesus is Lord and believe in your heart that God raised him from the dead, you will be saved' (Rom. 10: 9). That is, a confession of faith in Jesus as Lord must be made before one can be a Christian at all. The mouth must put its vote on record: Yes, Jesus is Lord, and Jesus is my Lord. Christ seems to have gone out of His way to make people come out into the open. For instance, the woman who has been healed through touching the hem of His garment so discreetly, and is now about to slip quietly away: in spite of the urgency of impatient Jairus, eager that Jesus should get to his dying daughter, He insists on halting the crowd and asking who had touched Him. Was He unaware of what had happened, or was He trying to embarrass the woman? Of course, neither of these things. The woman must be made to confess her shame and need and hopelessness which brought her to Him, and then to declare the wonder of her newly healed body. This was both a blessing to her, and to those who heard (Mk. 5: 24–34). However embarrassing it might be for this shy woman, her faith must be publicly confessed.

We are specifically told that the members of the Jerusalem church were all scattered by persecution, and only the apostles somehow remained there (Acts 8: 1), and that it was those who were scattered who 'went about preaching the word' (verse 4). That is, it was not only the apostles themselves commissioned by Christ, but every disciple and subsequent convert who went around telling

[6] A device used by workers among illiterates in which black, red and white coloured pages are used to speak of sin, atonement and cleansing.

others about Jesus. There is all the difference in the world between the evangelism of a church where the only gospel preaching is done by one man for one hour in a week inside a building, and the evangelism of a church which is done by a hundred men and women at all hours of the day, every day of the week, all over the city. Until the church of God gets back this same crusading spirit, with 'every Christian a revolutionary', it will not be behaving like the church of God.

But you say: I cannot preach, I cannot explain my faith to others. The answer to that, surely, is that you *must*. This is what you became a Christian for: not merely for your own personal enjoyment of salvation, but in order to bear the good news of Christ everywhere. You were asked not merely to be a spectator or some kind of subscriber, but a member of the team, an active revolutionary against the domination of evil and sin, seeking to liberate men and women from its power. Becoming a Christian is not like joining a comfortable kind of eternal Friendly Society, but more like enlisting in an army geared for total war demanding fanatical effort.

But if it helps, this sense of inadequacy about speaking is very common. Thus the youthful Jeremiah says, 'I do not know how to speak . . .' and puts it down to his youth. He seems to have the idea that loquaciousness increases with age, which is sometimes true; but the Lord sees his need differently and says to him, 'Do not say, "I am only a youth"; for to all to whom I send you you shall go, and whatever I command you you shall speak. Be not afraid of them, for *I am with you* to deliver you, says the Lord.' Then Jeremiah continues, 'Then the Lord put forth his hand and touched my mouth . . .' (Je. 1: 6–9). The hindrance was not his youth, but fear of the people to whom he would go. The promise is that he will not be alone, but that the Lord will be with him, and that his empty mouth will be filled with words from God.

Jeremiah was, as we can see from the book as a whole,

an extremely sensitive character, to whom it cost a great deal to speak for God. Yet he cannot be silent; even when he feels it would be more tactful to say nothing and so avoid criticism and opposition, he cannot keep quiet. 'The word of the Lord has become for me a reproach and derision all day long. If I say, "I will not mention him, or speak any more in his name," there is in my heart as it were a burning fire shut up in my bones, and I am weary with holding it in, and I cannot' (Je. 20: 8, 9). God grant that we too may have a 'burning fire' in our hearts, so that we must speak for Him; so that, like Paul, we may cry, 'Woe to me if I do not preach the gospel!' (1 Cor. 9: 16).

The young Ezekiel sees a vision of God and he is told, 'You shall speak my words to them, whether they hear or refuse to hear . . .' and then he is told to open his mouth and eat what he is given. And he is given a little scroll with God's word on it to eat (Ezk. 2: 7ff.). Then what God has given him and taught him, he can pass on to others. It is interesting that Isaiah, Jeremiah and Ezekiel all had some experience connected with their mouths— a burning coal to cleanse it, the hand of God to fill it, the word of God to feed it—to commission them for a life of service.

Moses also sought to avoid speaking for God and to excuse himself from any responsibility, as we have seen. 'Oh, my Lord, I am not eloquent . . . but I am slow of speech and of tongue.' Many of us will probably want to echo these words of Moses, feeling them to be true of ourselves, but the Lord says, 'Who has made man's mouth? Who makes him dumb, or deaf, or seeing, or blind? Is it not I, the Lord? Now therefore go, and I will be with your mouth and teach you what you shall speak' (Ex. 4: 10–12).

That is, what we cannot do in our strength or with our own ability, God promises to do. The Holy Spirit in the New Testament is seen as the inspirer of Christian utterance, and God promises still that He will help us to speak for Him. Peter, the fisherman, and John were judged by others to be 'uneducated, common men' (Acts 4: 13), but at the same time those others wondered at their boldness and recognized that the only reason which would account for it was that they had been with Jesus. It is this same Peter who urges those who speak to do so 'as one who utters oracles of God', and clearly this was his own approach. What matters is not the eloquence of the one who speaks, but the greatness of the One whose message he brings.

The Lord wants men and women through whom He can speak to other men and women, people who will pray and look for opportunities to speak of Him to others in the course of their daily lives. Are we prepared to give Him our mouths for this?

The girl with the golden voice

In Grimm's fairy-tale called 'The Three Little Men in the Wood' we meet two girls. One is sweet and obedient, and she is sent out on a freezing day, in just a paper cloak and with a crust of bread, to find strawberries. She shares her crust with the three little men and obeys their command to go out and sweep the snow, and there finds the strawberries. Her selfish step-sister goes out after her in a fur cloak, with a lovely picnic lunch which she refuses to share with the three little men, whose request to sweep she also refuses and, of course, she finds no strawberries. The first girl is rewarded by them, not only with increasing beauty and the promise of marriage to a king, but every time she opens her mouth—gold coins fall out! The step-sister is rewarded with increasing ugliness, and every time she opens her mouth—a toad jumps out.

What comes out of our mouths, golden coins or toads?

153

'The mouth of the righteous is a fountain of life . . . The tongue of the righteous is choice silver' (Pr. 10: 11, 20). We Christians are to be like the girl with the golden voice, whose speech is so helpful, apt and gracious that it is like a shower of gold coins. 'Let no evil talk come out of your mouths, but only such as is good for edifying, as fits the occasion, that it may impart grace to those who hear' (Eph. 4: 29).

This contrast between the two uses of the mouth is a constant theme of Scripture. The mouth of the upright delivers men, rather than trapping them in evil (Pr. 12: 6). The tongue of the wise brings healing, unlike the wounding and hurtful words like sword thrusts (Pr. 12: 18). Pleasant words are like a honeycomb, sweetness to the soul and health to the body (Pr. 16: 24). There is all the difference in the world between the words which wound and hurt, spread rumour and half-truth, and those which please, strengthen, encourage and build up. With words we may not only tell others of Christ, but may help and encourage our fellow Christians, and share with them our vision for serving the Lord. We may help those who have failed and need fellowship and encouragement. We need a mouth that is filled with golden words which give glory to God and may hasten the coming of His kingdom.

Fellowship, in the real meaning of the word

Christians often seem to use the word 'fellowship' to describe drinking tea and eating buns among believers! We have spoken already of the reticence of people to speak about Christ, and have seen that this often springs from a poverty of Christian experience, a fear of revealing our spiritual vacuum and a realization of the hypocrisy of forced and unnatural pious talk.

'Then they that feared the Lord spake often one to

another' (Mal. 3: 16, AV). It should be easier to speak of Christ inside the family with other Christians than to speak of Him to those whose reception may be disinterested, even hostile. If we cannot speak about our spiritual experience with fellow Christians, the probability is that we do not say much to non-Christians either. We have already tried to see how this matter of the frozen mouth can be dealt with through prayer for opportunities. It seems tragic that we Christians should merely 'talk' instead of communicating meaningfully with each other about our faith and the problems we find in applying it in daily life. Nobody wants to be an ostentatious promoter of pious conversation, but so often it is the little question or comment which acts as a kind of catalyst to precipitate a positive conversation, or a rudder that steers a discussion into more profitable channels. Unless there is this deeper level of communication among us, we are not really benefiting as we should from being a member of the Christian family. That we should live in a state of estrangement and loneliness even in the Christian crowd is a tragedy indeed.

There is never harm in being real, and to admit to barrenness or dryness or spiritual failure may be the first step to recovery of fruitfulness. It is hard for Christians to pray effectively for one another when they are ignorant of the other person's deepest needs and problems. James was definitely on to something when he wrote (literally) 'Keep on confessing (Present Middle Imperative) your faults to one another' and went on to urge that prayer could then be made (Jas. 5: 16). The Holy Spirit thus commands us to do this. It is an order, and the fact that some groups have overstressed confessing their faults, or not regulated it, so that it was misused, should not cause us to disregard this command. There is great blessing in small groups of Christians making their real problems known in an appropriate manner and praying for each other realistically. It is particularly in matters like sloth or timidity, spiritual barrenness or gossip, that such fellowship in speaking together can be a real help.

Suggestions for prayer and meditation

Is my mouth being used to commend Christ to other people, or do I keep silent?

Why do I not have more to say, and find more opportunities for witness?

Is it that there is no overflow of my heart in love for Christ?

Is there a need for cleansing, that my mouth may be opened again?

How much do I know about spontaneous praising of the Lord?

Have we prayed that the Lord will give us the ability to speak, have we asked Him to give us a commission to speak with others for Him?

Have we asked for a 'burning fire' in our hearts that will make us speak?

This last week, have there been 'gold' words or 'toad' words?

In my home am I really communicating, or just talking? Make a list of people to whom I might speak about Christ and faith in Him.

Pray for these people and for opportunity to speak naturally about Him to them.

Do I tend to use stereotyped jargon, which people do not understand, and which puts them off? Why not ask the Lord's help in expressing His gospel clearly?

Dear Lord, I want You to take my mouth and cleanse it, and fill it with loving helpful words which may be a blessing to others. Please use my mouth to bring others to hear Your word and respond to it. Please use my mouth to encourage my fellow Christians. For Jesus' sake.

9 CAREER or VOCATION?

Take my life and let it be
Consecrated, Lord, to Thee.

We have just one life to live. We may already have used
a quarter of it, a third of it, half of it, perhaps even more.
That part of it has gone, like Clementine, for ever. But
what about the part we have left? What are we going
to do with that? There is a very real possibility that we
may merely add a set of Christian convictions and habits,
and yet continue much as we always have done without
asking ourselves any such questions about the purpose of
living.

The accepted pattern

Most of us have very little say about what happens to
us during the earlier part of our lives. When we were
children other people settled what we should do. We had
no important decisions to make ourselves. Others decided
what school we should attend, where we should go for
our holidays, and so on. Some decisions were made by yet
others on the basis of examinations which others had
decided that we should take. Some people may even reach
the university and their mid-twenties without really ever
having made a major decision for themselves; their secondary school had told them to sit an entrance examination
for college, and so they did.

There are two choices, however, which are increasingly left to the individual himself to decide. This not so universally, for in some countries these major decisions are still taken by the parents, but in the late teens many of us start making the two major decisions of life: our life partner and our life work. Often we are not really mature enough or well enough informed to make these important choices for ourselves, and may just muddle along until some kind of arrangements have been arrived at. It can be rather a haphazard business. Fortunately in many countries decisions about a life partner have to be delayed until we are more mature, just for financial considerations. In other countries also the family still have considerable say in the choice of a life partner, so that some objective opinions about suitability and compatibility may be had.

The important decision about the direction of our life in terms of our major employment or our career may be settled by a family business connection, by some professional tradition, by the school which we attend, by our first job after leaving school or by the professional training which we obtained, partly by our own personal choice and partly through the encouragement of our parents and teachers. In the student world, some seem to be able to get within a few weeks of graduation without knowing what they are going to do afterwards. But the vast majority of people find that the general direction is set in the late teens or early twenties, even if the details and the extent of success and advancement only develop with the years. Some gifted individuals seem to be able to chop and change around in later life, but for good or ill the matter is usually settled somewhere between fifteen and twenty-five. Thereafter lie ahead perhaps some forty or fifty years of working life, a period of retirement with increasing loss of faculties, and then our life is over. What will we have to show for it? Will it be measured by life's little rewards and successes, some certificates of education, some silver cups indicative of athletic prowess, a few medals, some newspaper cuttings, promotion within our profession, some status in the local community, a presentation clock on retirement, an obituary notice and a well-attended funeral? Is that all that our life will have meant?

A fresh assessment

Do we now find ourselves doing whatever we are doing, for what now, from a Christian point of view, seem to be rather inadequate reasons: the financial rewards, the security of the pension on retirement, the status which the profession gives, genuine personal enthusiasm for the work involved, or from mere force of necessity? When a person becomes a Christian all these motives and attitudes will have to be rethought and reconsidered. We may, up to this point, have regarded our lives as our own. Certainly, looking back, we realize that really we had very little choice in the matter, and we have still less now: specialized training in a particular field, entry into a particular firm, our commitment to support aged parents, wife and children. Yet, none the less, we regard our lives as our own to do with as we like. But not any longer. '. . . you are no longer your own masters. A great price was paid to ransom you; glorify God by making your bodies the shrines of his presence' (1 Cor. 6: 19, 20, Knox).

As we have seen, the Christian regards himself as a slave of Jesus Christ, and all that he does needs to be seen in this new light. Previously I was in rebellion, shaking my fist at God and the world: 'My life's my own, isn't it?' But not any longer. I have laid down my arms of rebellion, cast myself on His mercy and entered His service. He has made me a member of His household, so that now I am His slave ready to obey His orders, however they may conflict with what I have hitherto regarded as my personal self-interest. This means that I have to rethink my whole attitude to what I am doing with this one life that I have. My future career may still be un-settled, and there may be before me a whole range of possibilities about which I must seek to know my new Master's will. In some cases, if I am still at the student stage, an earlier decision may have to be reconsidered according to the principles set out in the following sections.

A new attitude or a new assignment?

Does becoming a Christian mean that I contemplate changing my life work? Or only changing my attitude to the one I have? What are the biblical principles? The same principles hold if someone has been converted before a final decision has been made about the future working life, and is weighing up the possibilities. They would also be applicable in the case of a Christian woman who recog-nizes that later her professional life may be terminated or interrupted by the Lord leading her to marriage and the raising of a family.

1. *Aim for the place of maximum usefulness*

Nearly any job undertaken whole-heartedly in the right Christian spirit may be enjoyable and rewarding and useful. There are possibly many callings in which we could glorify God through the work that we do. It is important that we should have such a Christian attitude to the work which we are doing.[1] But it seems that there is more than this at stake and it is of crucial importance, especially in seeking God's will for our lives in terms of a career, or rather of our calling from God. That is, what is the place of maximum usefulness for me? I have certain strong points and certain weak points, but with all my gifts and with all my limitations where can I be most

[1] See also my *Consistent Christianity* (IVF, 1960), pp. 26ff.

use to the Lord, and how can I please Him most? Perhaps I have various commitments already in terms of wife and children, and I have to be useful to them as well as to society at large. Both are part of my service for God. But how can I be most use to God and most blessing to other people? Any Christian will, if he is the kind of whole-hearted fellow we are writing about, turn his mind to serving the Lord through what he is doing; but more than that, what is the most effective deployment of what God has made me? Where can I exert maximum leverage for the glory of God and extension of His kingdom? Where can I do most damage to the devil and the most good to the church of God?

This is not for one moment intended to suggest that a person cannot be at their maximum usefulness unless their work has some obvious 'religious' connection. If the work we are doing is in terms of good government, the setting of honest standards in commerce and industry, the production of that which is pleasing and glorifying to God in terms of good craftsmanship (and this list might be prolonged almost indefinitely), then, it may be, that is the place of maximum usefulness for us. Quite apart from the value of the personal contacts that it gives us with people, there is an intrinsic value in the work itself as part of God's common grace to men. In any case the stationing and deployment of Christians in strategic places through society, where they may be the salt of the earth preserving it from corruption, is also of great importance. It is this kind of work which may be the place of maximum usefulness. But we must always question, am I in a place of usefulness? And more than that, am I in the place of my maximum usefulness? One thing we may be certain of is that God has a chosen place for us, 'good works, which God prepared beforehand, that we should walk in them' (Eph. 2: 10), and we need to ask Him to show us what that work chosen by Him should be. In the same way we shall need periodically to reassess whether we are still in that place of maximum usefulness, or whether a change might not stir us up to meet fresh challenges with renewed energy and incentive.

2. *Remain in the calling wherein you are called*

'Every one should remain in the state in which he was called. Were you a slave when called? Never mind. But if you can gain your freedom, avail yourself of the opportunity. . . . So, brethren, in whatever state each was called, there let him remain with God' (1 Cor. 7: 20–24). Paul here states the general principles. Becoming a Christian is no reason to give up what you are doing before you came to Christ. The Lord has had His hand upon us for longer than we know. Paul presumably learnt the trade of tent-making before ever he was a Christian, but it stood him in good stead when he had to work to support himself for a preaching ministry. Aquila and Priscilla were not called to stop making tents when they were converted. An outstanding example is Onesimus, the slave of Philemon, who had run away and found Christ when sharing a prison with Paul (who, incidentally, found a way to make even the 'vocation' of being a prisoner glorifying to God). Paul sends him back to his former master to work again as a slave, though now as a Christian slave of a Christian master in expectation of a very different kind of relationship, and with a very different attitude to his work. The Roman centurion Cornelius (Acts 10) and the Roman proconsul Sergius Paulus (Acts 13) presumably continued in their respective professions after conversion. Certainly, at Philippi, it seems that Lydia would have continued with her textile business, and the meetings of the church there must always have had the characteristic odour of the bales of purple cloth stacked there for sale. We may assume that the gaoler continued his work in the city prison in Philippi, but treated his prisoners more

kindly after finding that he had imprisoned 'angels unawares'.

The strength of a church lies in its members in common
occupations. It is interesting to compare the churches in
Korea and Japan, and to wonder why one has prospered
so much more than the other. There are, of course, many
contributory causes, but one cannot help wondering
whether the so-called Nevius Method, that is the indi-
genous church principles suggested by Nevius who was a
veteran China missionary, had not a great deal to do with
it. The first principle was expressed like this: 'Let each
man abide in the calling wherein he was found, teaching
that each was to be an individual worker for Christ, and
to live Christ in his own neighbourhood, supporting himself by his trade.'[2] So today in Korea every Christian is
a Christian worker, seeking to evangelize in his own
neighbourhood (at home or work), and is supported by
his own labours. In Japan the church never seems to
have been so centred in its laymen, but to have depended
upon its full-time workers to an extent which has ham-
pered its witness. The Korean church has also been a
persecuted church for much of its history. A lay-centred
church is hard to destroy, but in Japan, if you were to
make everyone work on Sundays, put the pastors in prison
and use the church buildings for some other purpose, such
as warehouses, *etc.*, one wonders just how much would
be able to continue.

An interesting testimony to the value of such lay-
centred Christian activity comes from Communist China.
'The church was declared a "reactionary group" and
closed by government order. But the congregation although scattered began to gather in small groups in
houses, while continuing to petition the municipal and
central governments to restore their church to them. It
was decided officially that to give them back their church

[2] Kun Sam Lee, *Christian Confrontation with Shinto Nationalism*,
p. 156.

would be better than to run the risk of multiplying clandestine "underground home congregations".[3]

You may be able to lock up the Christian pastors, who are often marked men in times of persecution, but you cannot lock up every single Christian, nor prevent them from speaking to others. It was this kind of church which survived the terrible persecutions of the Roman Empire, and the importance of every Christian working and witnessing within his own calling cannot be overemphasized.

3. *Some must change their profession when they are converted*

Although Lydia and the gaoler may have continued in their respective callings, the third convert at Philippi, for it seems that she was such (Acts 16), must have changed her calling. She had been a 'pythoness'; like the Delphi priestesses, she had a spirit of divination, which was being used by her masters for profit. When Paul cast out this spirit, her employers saw that 'their hope of gain was gone' and there ensued a riot which led to the imprisonment of the apostles and the conversion of the gaoler and his family. The girl clearly could not continue in her profession. It must also have been true of Crispus, who had been a ruler of the synagogue in Corinth, and of Sosthenes who succeeded him, and who, if he is the same one whose name is joined with Paul in the address to that church, appears also to have been converted. They may have had other employment, but they could not continue as synagogue officers now that they were Christians. The same presumably also held for the 'great company of the priests' (Acts 6: 7) who believed. The nature of their work was such that it had to be changed once they had come to Christ.

'Let him that stole steal no more' may be an extreme case of the necessity for a changed vocation, but it reminds

[3] Article by George Patterson in *Christianity Today*, July 1965, on information from defected member of Religious Affairs Bureau.

us that there are professions which are barred to Christians. There are some which are not so disreputable or accepted as criminal, which may even be regarded as respectable and remunerative occupations, but which are non-productive occupations deriving profit from the cupidity or foolishness of their fellow men.

4. Some may be called out for full-time service

Let it be stressed again that because one has become a Christian, though all of us are to be full-time Christians, and all of us are to be whole-heartedly engaged in propagating the gospel, there is no need to feel that wholeheartedness must result in a man throwing up his present means of livelihood in order to enter the ministry, or that this calling is to be revered above other callings.

The pre-Reformation period thought of the 'religious life' as demanding retirement from the sinful world; only the full-time 'religious' could live a life truly pleasing to God, and even in these more enlightened days you may still hear Roman Catholic radio programmes glorifying the celibate life as being more exalted than the married one, and speaking approvingly of married people who forsake their partners in order to serve Christ in a monastery. The Reformation established the doctrine of a calling and a priesthood of all believers. Holiness is to be manifested not in the monastery but in marriage; not in poverty but in productivity; not in begging alms but in giving them; not in fleeing from sex but by using it for God's glory; not in living a single life in holy isolation, but, if a single life is His will for us, in living a life of involvement in the world, brushing shoulders with the needy millions. We are no longer restricted to a special holy class; all Christians are called to be saints, and all Christians have a vocation from God.

Oddly enough, in spite of this Reformation heritage, there still hangs on the idea, even among Protestants, that to be some kind of professional worker is a higher calling than others. The fact remains that this is God's calling for some. People may be called to Christ and be converted at all stages of life, in youth, middle or old age. It is also true that a man may be called to so-called full-time service at any time. Some are called in later life, such as Matthew called from the tax office, and later his friend Zacchaeus, who seems to have been a Chief Tax Inspector, or the several fishermen disciples. Others, such as Timothy, seem to have been called while they were quite young (Acts 16: 1–13). He appears to be an example of someone who was called to full-time service early, before he had entered any other calling.

However, it is interesting to note that, in general, in New Testament times it is older men who were appointed to leadership of the local churches, while the younger men, whose example is quoted, seemed to have had more of an itinerant, or what today one would think of as a missionary, ministry. These days the balance seems to have been upset. Men are put in charge of local churches, who have, it is true, some academic qualifications, but who have little experience of much outside of student life. This seems in marked contrast to the New Testament pattern (*cf.* 1 Tim. 3: 1–13, where qualifications for local leadership are given), which places less emphasis on the academic training and more on being an established married man, with a well-disciplined household, and standing in society in his own merit.[4]

However, the inadequacy of all but the most exceptional callow youths for the oversight of local churches is being increasingly recognized, and in some countries there seems to be an increasing number of older, experienced men entering full-time service. Such a trend must be welcomed as a return to a more scriptural position from one influenced by more pre-Reformation outlooks, and also as

[4] This is well developed in Roland Allen, *The Ministry of the Spirit* (World Dominion Press, 1962), p. 160, in the section called The Case for Voluntary Clergy.

one which in the middle years entails very genuine sacrifice in terms of income and living standards. Thus, while it may not be that we shall be called to the ministry in our twenties, we may be in our thirties, and perhaps, ideally, in our forties and fifties. Are we prepared for this?

Have we considered it?

Having said all this, there *is* a need for those in full-time ministry, both younger men and older men. This is not really a matter for volunteers: some very unsuitable people may volunteer for the ministry, as we all know, though fortunately the majority of the most unsuitable ones get weeded out. We shall always have a sneaking suspicion about some volunteers, and perhaps about ourselves if we were volunteers, that we are doing this only because we do not have the ability to do anything else. It is sadly true in some parts of the world that many of the young candidates for the ministry in the theological colleges are drawn from mission school pupils who have failed to get entry into the high school or university. It is the mission school failures who are pushed into the ministry. This also reflects a failure on the part of some of those who do succeed academically to be willing to forgo the monetary and social advantages of their education and enter the ministry. And so you get the tragic situation of a professional ministry of a lower intellectual standard, while those who might have ministered are not prepared for the sacrifice involved, and can only criticize the ministry from without for its admitted shortcomings. All this indicates the breakdown of what we call the volunteer method. It was never a scriptural one in any case.

The biblical pattern seems to be that a man's gifts and abilities are recognized by others in the church, for he is already using these gifts in the local church in some way or another, and then the suggestion is made by them that he has the various qualities needed for leadership in the church. He may be an older man, highly successful in his own profession, with some standing in the community at large: so much the better if he is. A study of the Book of the Acts shows no evidence of any volunteer system at all: men are chosen and sent. Thus Peter and John were sent to Samaria (8: 14), and Barnabas to Antioch (11: 22) by the Jerusalem church. Barnabas went and drew Saul into the work in Antioch (11: 26), and it was after prayer and seeking of the Lord's will by all the leaders of this new church that the two of them were sent out as missionaries (13: 1–4). Paul and Barnabas were later sent to Jerusalem with some others (15: 2) by the church at Antioch, and later the church at Jerusalem sent Judas, Barnabas and Silas to Antioch (15: 22). It was after this that we read 'Paul chose Silas' (15: 40) and 'Paul wanted Timothy to accompany him' (16: 3). What emerges from this is that, while no doubt a man might have a personal conviction that it was the Lord's will for him, it was never this factor alone which resulted in men going out in 'full-time work'. Others always took the initiative and a man was chosen by his brethren in his own church, or at least commended by them and chosen by someone already actively engaged in the ministry.

Such an approach demands a proper sense of responsibility among Christians. It is not only a question of what *I* can do (which might be just wild, irresponsible, extroverted individualism), but of what *we* do? William Carey had a deep conviction about the need to preach the gospel to the heathen, but he was eager to carry his brethren with him. In other words, there is a need for a much deeper sense of corporate responsibility, to decide together as a group of Christians, about when an individual among them should be called to the full-time ministry. This kind of approach solves a great deal in the matter of support in prayer and finance. If a man has gone into full-time work because of the united conviction of his fellow Christians that this is the Lord's will, then they will naturally feel the need to support him in prayer and to supply his physical needs.

The heading of this section, then, 'Have we considered it?', is in the plural for this very good reason, that this kind of decision about a man or a woman's fitness for full-time service needs to be made by Christians as a praying group. It is in one sense a return to the family principle, which, as we have seen, still governs in some measure a man's career, and in some countries his marriage as well. There is thus something very fitting and appropriate about the new family, the local community of Christians, having this joint sense of responsibility. What we need is not just a lot of odd individuals who are burning with zeal and a desire to serve Christ, but whole congregations of people, with such a passion to serve Christ together. The minister has a great responsibility not only to encourage every individual in the church to get into action (instead of regarding himself as the source of all action), but also to encourage the church together as a team to go all out in their own district and wherever they can make an impact.

The same, of course, is true of Christian Unions. There is a danger that only the elected committee feel responsible, while the remainder merely attend meetings arranged by 'the CU' thought of as something existing apart from themselves, and exercise a passive or critical spectator role from the touchline, instead of realizing that they are in the team and expected to get in and shove. The test of good leadership is not its ability to do the organizing work, so much as the ability to mobilize every available person and get them into action. It is in such vital, living fellowships that we may look for an increase of men being sent out into full-time ministry.

There is still the challenge to the individual to be willing, if the Lord so show him, and so lead his brethren to urge him to such a course, to leave his chosen profession and perhaps his financial security, not only in his youth, but also to have this same adventurous spirit throughout life, even in the middle years. It is something which we need to consider. These decisions are not, in the New Testament, purely individual decisions, and it may well be that there are those among us to whom a word in season might be in order. Certainly it seems to be the kind of thing that a live church will be praying about.

To the end of the earth

This responsibility of Christians corporately does not, however, end with the local activity centred on that one building where the church meets for worship, or the manifold extensions of it that may meet in houses throughout the area always pressing out and seeking to win others for the Lord. Missionary activity seems to occupy an odd niche in the homeland churches; it all seems quaintly unreal. After all the more interesting announcements, there comes the final notice, with a kind of in-case-anyone-happens-to-be-interested diminuendo, of the forthcoming visit of the deputation speaker from the Back of Beyond Missionary Union, who will give a lantern lecture on Colporteurs in Carparthia. When Christopher Robin grows up a bit it would seem quite in place for him to muddle along through his prayers saying, 'Oh! God bless Missions—I quite forgot.' Pious generalities and polite interest seem about as much as some are prepared to give to missionary work.

But why do we pray 'Thy kingdom come, Thy will be done . . .', unless that involves obedience to commands like 'Go . . . and make disciples of all nations . . .? So often missionary work seems to involve praying for people we have never met and giving to sets of initials representing missionary societies, instead of real living involvement in what is going on. Following what we have already tried to say about corporate responsibility, does it not also mean that, recognizing this command to us as His people to take the gospel to all nations, we get together as a fellowship and say, 'Lord, what can we do about this? Is there anyone or two or three or more people among us with the gifts for such work? Are there any we can send out?' If a church sends out, then there is no problem about prayer and support. These folk have gone out as representatives of the church; it is the work not just of the individuals but of the group, and of course they will pray for them and of course they will give for their support. This will not be just taking collections and letting them get along as best they can, but realistically working out how much it will cost them to live out there, and seeking to provide it. After all, it is our fault that they are out there; we sent them, we are responsible, we are vitally concerned.

The tragedy so often is that missionary concern is the concern of so few, of the few extra-fanatical people in the church who have time for extra meetings, which often means the older people, when it ought to be the concern of *all*. Concern for missionary work ought not to be some kind of quaint excrescence added to other church activity, but it ought to be regarded as an indispensable mark of Christian maturity and holiness. Show me a man who is really a mature Christian, and that man will have a burning concern for missionary work all over the world.

There are still areas needing pioneer evangelists. For the most part the Moslem world is unevangelized; so are huge areas of pagan Europe; so are the rural areas in many parts of the world; and so increasingly in these days of growing urbanization are the great industrial areas. There are not only geographical areas, but also social strata which are unevangelized and need pioneers: people to work among medicals, among nurses, among the professional classes, among the working masses. Whether such workers go supported financially from home, or supporting themselves by using their own qualifications, there is still a need for evangelists, teachers of evangelists, and others to work alongside the existing national churches, often still weak and struggling. A little study of church history also seems to show that, while an effective witness may be established in one generation, for one reason and another that work may become ineffective and a country have to be evangelized all over again in the next. To talk of the evangelization of the world in this generation is a fine thing, but what of the next generation?

Don't potter

'Take my life.' What about yours? Do you have a sense of purpose and direction in your Christian life, determined to use these years for Jesus Christ? Or are you still pottering aimlessly about, wondering what a Christian is here for anyway? You may potter faithfully up and down to attend church every week, but what are you doing for the Lord and for His kingdom? We have this one life to live, perhaps to fourscore years (and perhaps not so long). Will we do something for the Lord which will stand for eternity, something which will last? Or will we just potter?

There was a student once who took first-class honours in Mathematics and the leading university Classics prize into the bargain. He seemed all set for a brilliant academic career. He chose to get ordained as a curate in an unpopular evangelical church. Well, he could still move on to a comfortable south coast parish, and one day, perhaps, to a bishopric. At twenty-four years of age he set out for India; it took him almost a year to get there. He died at the age of thirty-one. But before that happened he had produced translations of the New Testament in three languages—Hindustani, Arabic and Persian. He did something before he coughed out what was left of his short life in the burning heat of the Persian desert. He didn't potter. When he sailed he had only a quarter of his life left—but he did something with it.

Two days before he died it happened that his portrait arrived in Cambridge, some thousands of miles away, back to the church where he had been curate, and to Charles Simeon its minister. They unpacked the portrait and hung it up, that picture of Henry Martyn. Simeon said that those eyes used to look down at him from the picture and that they seemed to say, 'Don't trifle. Don't trifle.' That same picture is still hanging in a hall where students pray every day that the Lord will use them and use their lives for His glory, and the eyes that look down on them from the picture still seem to say, 'Don't trifle.' Or, in other words, 'Don't potter.'

Suggestions for prayer and meditation

Is my life given to the Lord for Him to use, in whatever way He pleases?

Am I prepared to continue in my present calling, using every opportunity to serve Him?

Would I be prepared to leave it, even in middle life, to serve the church of Christ?

Is there anything I can do, not only to dedicate myself wholly to the Lord, but to encourage others in the church to do the same, and together to work all out as hard as we can for Him?

Is missionary work a kind of Cinderella in my thinking, or do I put it in the forefront of my thinking, as part of my individual and corporate responsibility as a Christian?

174

Are there any missionary magazines I might take in order to enlarge my vision?

Is there any prayer group I have been refraining from joining?

Could I perhaps help to back up one particular missionary in prayer?

Am I done with pottering? If not, when will I stop?

Lord, show me what I can do and give me the strength to do it.

10 ACTIVISM or EMPOWERING?

*Take myself, and I will be
Ever, only, all for Thee.*

The aim of this book is to urge action. We have tried to make it plain that being a Christian means that we are, by definition, called to action. We are not to be passive spectators of 'religion', content with a weekly appearance in 'church', but we are to devote all our energy, gifts, intellect and imagination to the passionate service of Christ. We are to love God with all our heart, and soul, and mind, and strength. It is not enough to carry our Bible with us to church, where we may be instructed in the faith, but it must be translated into terms of daily living and enthusiastic obedience, into dynamic, loving service. There should be a passion and a sense of abandonment to the Lord and to His service.

There is nothing new about all this; there have been plenty of other books saying the same thing. For example, *God's Frozen People*[1] has shown very clearly how a false doctrine of the ministry has tended to shut up the laity to a passive role. But the basic problem is not really organizational, but spiritual. It is not enough to say to each other, 'You must go out and evangelize for Christ . . . ,' because the man in the pulpit has been saying it to the man in the pew for years, and has gone on saying it faithfully, even when he begins to despair of

[1] M. Gibbs and T. R. Morton, *God's Frozen People* (Fontana, 1964).

anyone taking any notice. How can you get everybody mobilized? How can you get Christians to live in the kind of way the Bible says that we should? It is one thing for us to feel frustrated with ourselves and with everybody else for not being what we know we ought to be. But when we have something of the vision of the church of God as the living, dynamic thing that it ought to be, how can this be brought to pass?

You can do nothing

There is a danger in a book of this kind, that it will over-emphasize man. The last thing we want is a kind of whirl of furious activism—even more meetings, even more committees—which is just in terms of organization and activity only. If the Holy Spirit were taken away from the church, as the Shekinah Glory departed from the temple in Ezekiel's vision (Ezk. 11: 22ff.), one wonders if a great deal of our meetings and activities would not continue unaltered. In other words, as somebody else put it, a great deal of church activity can be attributed to natural rather than to supernatural causes. They are just carried on as a matter of convention and established custom without reliance on the Holy Spirit at all. It has been for this reason that this book has sought to encourage its readers not merely to read, but at the end of each chapter to pray, and to seek the blessing and help of God's Holy Spirit at every stage of our thinking.

The Bible says, 'You can do nothing.' But one needs a bit more context, or this sentence can be very discouraging. What the Lord Jesus said was, 'Without me, you can do nothing.'

He likened the Christian, trying to 'do without' God, to a branch cut off from the tree, withering away and fit for nothing but burning. There is nothing you can do with a fruitless vine except burn it, for there is no com-

mercial use even for the wood of it (Ezk. 15.) It is an
extraordinary twist of ideas that we have recently had
propagated in the churches the idea that God is teaching
us to 'Do without Him'. (The exact quotation is, 'God is
teaching us that we must live as men who can get along
very well without him,'[2] though one recognizes that in
the context Bonhoeffer may not have meant by that what
some have tried to say that he did.) There seems to be a
tendency, however, to say that we must get rid of all this
pietism and prayer and so on (except for a few weak souls
who need it as a prop). The Christian 'come of age' no
longer needs to set apart times for prayer.

A little reflection about the example of our Lord Jesus
will show that is a badly mistaken emphasis. Was our
Lord an immature man, a relic of an old-fashioned
approach to religion? Why, then, are we told constantly
that He was always retiring in order to pray? You cannot
miss it. (See, for example, Lk. 3: 21; 5: 16; 6: 12; 9: 18;
11: 1; 22: 41). He instructs us that we 'ought always to
pray and not lose heart' (Lk. 18: 1). Was the Lord Jesus
an unbalanced pietist, out of touch with the secular
world? Here rather is One known as the friend of publicans and sinners, and who constantly resorts to prayer. If
ever any person might have claimed constant communion
with God, and therefore have no reason for any set times
of prayer, surely it was the Lord Jesus. Yet He seems to
have regarded prayer as essential and He taught His disciples to do the same. Prayer is an essential recognition
of our own helplessness and dependence upon Him. We
need Him; we must feed on Him who is our life. We need
the supply, the help and encouragement, the under-
girding, the empowering of His Spirit. Without Him, we
can do nothing.

[2] D. Bonhoeffer, *Letters from Prison* (SCM Press, 1956), p. 122.

Full dependence

If this book is a call to action, then it is not to mere human activity, but rather to activation by the Holy Spirit of God. It is a call to pray first, and to act afterwards. It is a call to sit first at His feet, like Mary, to find out what He wants us to do, before we go bustling into action, like Martha, busy with a great deal of activity which He would rather we left (Lk. 10: 38–42).

We cannot act in accord with the will of God, unless we first take the trouble to find out what the will of God is. That certainly means an open ear to hear His promptings at all times, but it also means times set aside to study His revealed will in the Bible. If we cannot be bothered to discover what His will is, plainly revealed in Scripture, then it is sheer folly to expect it to be revealed in some other way. There is a danger, if we do not know what He has certainly and plainly revealed in the Bible, but think that it is more 'spiritual' to listen for intuitions of guidance, that we may mistake the promptings of the devil for the voice of the Spirit. (Jonathan Edwards, writing in 'Thoughts on Revival', says that Satan seeks to delude revived believers by immediate suggestions and inspirations, inviting them to conclude that the thoughts and texts which come into their mind unbidden must be messages from God.)

We must make sure that everything is in obedience to His revealed will. As we have seen, the essence of fanaticism is not to be over-biblical but to be not biblical enough. We need to set apart time to study His Word, to listen to His voice and to ask His help to obey and fulfil His commandments. You cannot work for God unless you allow Him to direct that work. You cannot fight for God unless your lines of communication with Him are properly established. You cannot bear fruit for Him unless you are in organic communion with Him. You

cannot work for God unless you work with God. It is not
enough to be active, unless it is the power of God which
activates us. It is not enough to be energetic unless He
energizes us.

'Unless our zeal be directed by the Spirit of God it will
be of no avail to plead on our behalf that we undertook
nothing but from proper zeal. But the Spirit Himself will
guide us by wisdom and prudence that we may do nothing
contrary to our duty or beyond our calling . . .' writes
Calvin (commenting on Lk. 9: 55). He is writing against
misdirected zeal, and speaks of moderation as a gift of
the Spirit, because he uses moderation in the sense of
discipline, temperance and self-control. Clearly that
which is mere fleshly zeal and not prompted by the Holy
Spirit is to be avoided, so that more than ever we need
to insist on both the empowering and the direction of
the Holy Spirit.

The Old Testament contains examples of people trying
to do 'without God', relying on their own strength and
meeting disaster in consequence. An outstanding example
is when the Israelites have been told that because of their
unbelief they may not enter the promised land now, because they refused to go up earlier. They then change
their minds and, although Moses warns them against it,
they make an attack and are scattered by the Amalekites
and Canaanites (Nu. 14: 40ff. and Dt. 1: 41ff.). God was
not in the midst of them and they should not have gone.
A similar problem was the tendency of Israel to trust in
expedient political alliances and worldly-wise policies instead of trusting in the Lord Himself. 'Woe to those who
go down to Egypt for help and rely on horses, who trust
in chariots because they are many and in horsemen because they are very strong, but do not look to the Holy
One of Israel or consult the Lord!' (Is. 31: 1).

The great contrast between human strength and divine
help is made by Jeremiah. 'Cursed is the man who trusts

in man and makes flesh his arm, whose heart turns away from the Lord. He is like a shrub in the desert, and shall not see any good come. He shall dwell in the parched places of the wilderness, in an uninhabited salt land. Blessed is the man who trusts in the Lord, whose trust is the Lord. He is like a tree planted by water, that sends out its roots by the stream, and does not fear when heat comes, for its leaves remain green, and is not anxious in the year of drought, for it does not cease to bear fruit' (Je. 17: 5–8). Action for God depends upon a living union with Him, our spiritual roots being nourished and supplied by the divine refreshing and strengthening. There is a danger in a Liberalism which has sought to eliminate supernatural interference from the Bible, for this means that neither can it expect any supernatural divine intervention in human experience, and man must help himself.

How to do it

But it is not only Liberals who have been in danger of overlooking the weakness of human ability, for Evangelicals have been guilty of a similar fault. If some have merely told the layman that he must act, others have seen the inadequacy of this and said that the solution is to be found in 'training', that is, he must be told 'how' to do it. We live in the days of 'how to do it' methodology. We are offered 'Soul-winning made easy'. How could it be easy and should it ever be so? Is the conversion of men and women to Christ merely a matter of ten easy lessons? Preach the gospel *this* way, we are told, and be sure of results. The trouble with all the patent methods is that they imply that, if the church had known this method from the beginning, all would have been well. It almost implies that, though the Bible is inspired, it has just failed to make this point sufficiently clear, but now here at last is the answer. But actually the problem is not solved even by the 'Ten Easy Steps' approach, for the steps still have to be taken, and it may be easier to outline what they are than actually to take them.

Recently somebody speaking of the excellence of the 'Evangelism in Depth' approach (and one would agree on its value, but stress the necessity of relying on the Holy Spirit and not upon the method in itself) argued that it was so good, that even the false sects can get comparable results using the same methods. What was that supposed to prove? It proves only that certain methods can be relied upon to produce 'results', which may be spurious, and can be explained in terms of purely natural causes in terms of the percentages who will respond to a certain type of approach. If the results can be guaranteed, even if the message is not a Christian message, then it would seem that they are not the result of the work of the Spirit.

'The weapons of our warfare are not worldly but have divine power to destroy strongholds' (2 Cor. 10: 4). Our methods are not to be just worldly methods, the application to evangelism of methods of business persuasion and advertising and good sales technique. Our methods are to be spiritual methods, based upon prayer and spiritual dependence upon the Holy Spirit. There is no merit in poor organization, or using methods which repel instead of attract, but we must repudiate the idea that success is merely a matter of using certain methods. The New Testament church used New Testament methods, for they knew of none other, and they were filled with the Holy Spirit; but they did not succeed in evangelizing the world in their own generation. The Lord Jesus Himself trained only twelve men. Are we to suggest that, if He had used 'better methods', He would have been more successful?

'Not by might, nor by power, but by my Spirit, says the Lord of Hosts' (Zc 4: 6). There is a tendency for us to rely upon organization, upon fund-raising and good finance, a good platform, famous names on a Council of

Reference, and so forth. But God has chosen the weak things of the world, the foolish, the nobodies, the people of no social status or intellectual gifts, to confound the things in which men so easily come to trust, in terms of reputation and status. If a man is much used of God, then so easily we expect the blessing of God just because that man is preaching, rather than because we too are trusting in the God who uses him. There is no substitute at all for the power of God. Mere organization, activity and committees may be more of a hindrance than a help.

'One problem all Christians face is our increasing isolation from the world, from our neighbours and associates who are not Christians. By monopolising our time, most of our Christian activities only increase our distance from others, even activities like International Gospel Blimps, Inc., that exist for an evangelistic purpose. We attend committee meetings, we serve on boards, we prepare dinners, we run the mimeograph, we organise and re-organise. And we end up without time to get to know our neighbours, let alone to love them. For love is doing, not feeling. Therefore love demands time.'[3] Mere Christian activism confined to Christian circles, so that we are just being busy about being busy, without real involvement with the non-Christian world around us, is one of the biggest weaknesses of evangelical Christianity; so often Christians have only minimal and superficial contacts with non-Christians.

What we are urging, then, is that we follow the will of Christ, rather than the will of men, which so often runs in terms of organizations and big schemes for this and that. As a result of committing themselves more whole-heartedly to Christ, the Lord might lead somebody to form some new society or organization (though we really seem to have enough already), but it might rather be that a Christian individual, in all the weakness and foolishness of somebody who is a nobody, not writing on any impres-

[3] J. T. Bayly, *The Gospel Blimp* (Victory Press, 1962), pp. 82, 83.

sively headed notepaper, or representing any impressive organization, should go out to do something for Jesus Christ.

Perhaps it may be to love your neighbour next door in some practical way, to visit the local hospital or the prison or the local old people's home. 'If our Gospel be hid in America today, it is hid to the negroes and other minority groups, to members of labour unions, to the unchurched, the poor, the unwanted,' Bayly goes on paraphrasing 2 Corinthians 4: 8, and it is not really a difficult exercise to paraphrase it to fit our own national scene, and those who seem to lie outside the pale of the church. It is interesting to note that often the best work is done by those who have no knowledge of the latest techniques and methods. Anybody who is determined to do something soon begins to find some method of doing it.

We are right to criticize 'religion' and modern 'institutional Christendom' (in all its self-preoccupation with the trivia of church politics, and tithing the mint, anise and cummin of its own shibboleths), providing we recognize our own personal involvement and responsibility for it. We do not help the situation by providing alternative human organizations and structures *ad infinitum*. ' "Woe to the rebellious children," says the Lord, "who carry out a plan, but not mine; who make a league, but not of my spirit . . ." ' (Is. 30: 1). The answer to a humanized church is not another man-devised solution. We must return to the biblical pattern both for the church and for the Christian individual. We must reform both our personal and corporate activity by the Word of God, and determine that it must be activated by Him, and that it will be by His power and not ours.

Full committal

Some Christians seem to lack joy as Christians. They do not seem to be in full enjoyment of Christian living, and one wonders if this is because they are not fully committed to the service of Christ. It may be, as we saw in the first chapter, that there is a fear of becoming a fanatic, but it is far more likely that there has not been a willingness to be fully surrendered to Christ. There is perhaps a sneaking fear that He might take mean advantage of us, and that we might miss the best in life. One has only to put it this way to show its absurdity: who can better direct my life than the Author of it? Perhaps we are afraid that, if we follow Him unconditionally, we may lose our lives. For He asks from us a spirit of abandonment to His service, a willingness to lose our lives for His sake and the gospel's (Mk. 8: 35). In other words, there needs to be a surrender of ourselves to Him: 'Lord, I am willing for anything You want me to do, wherever I have to go, at whatever personal cost to myself. I trust You and trust myself to You for service all the days of my life.' This is surely what Paul means when he utters those passionate words, 'that . . . always Christ will be honoured in my body, whether by life or by death' (Phil. 1: 20).

Ideally of course, as we have seen in chapter 2, this is something which should have been understood at the time of conversion; this is what is implied by calling Jesus 'Lord'. It means that we say 'Yes' to all His commands and all His demands. But sometimes this is not realized even partially at the time of conversion, and later we come to a crisis of dissatisfaction with our Christian lives, and the realization that we have been accepting God's blessings for our own convenience, and that we have never fully committed ourselves to the Lord for His service.

The Bible teaches two things about committal to His service. The first is that it is to be a once-for-all committal, and the second that it is to be an oft-repeated committal. This is not really a contradiction, for a wedding is a decisive, once-for-all committal, and yet it is continually realized and actualized by repeated committal to each other in marriage. A couple may even get married and only subsequently realize the full and glorious significance of it, in terms of whole-hearted loyalty to each other.

'Do not yield your members to sin as instruments of wickedness, but yield yourselves to God as men who have been brought from death to life, and your members to God as instruments of righteousness' (Rom. 6: 13). These words are addressed by Paul to the Christians at Rome. They are already Christians, but he urges them to surrender themselves to God, and the tense indicates that this is a once-for-all act. There is a change of tense from the idea of a repeated yielding to sin succumbing to temptation, to the aorist imperative meaning 'to dedicate by one decisive act, one resolute effort'.[4] In other words, Paul tells us that we are to surrender ourselves to Christ by a decisive act, and this includes our members, which we have spoken of in the earlier chapters in terms of hands and feet, our intellects, our mouths, our sex, our energies, all that we are—these are all to be given to Him. Elsewhere Paul speaks of the Macedonians giving 'themselves to the Lord' (2 Cor. 8: 5). The whole direction of this book is surely to bring us to this point of dedication, of giving ourselves to Christ for His service.

In the very same letter (so that we can be sure no contradiction was involved in the mind of Paul) we find a further exhortation, based on the earlier one. 'I appeal to you therefore, brethren, by the mercies of God, to present your bodies as a living sacrifice, holy and acceptable to God, which is your spiritual worship' (Rom. 12: 1). Here the meaning is to go on presenting yourself by repeated acts of dedication, like the daily offering in the temple. The old sacrifices involved the offering of the body of an animal; now it is to be our own. Then it was

[4] W. Sanday and A. C. Headlam, *Romans* (*International Critical Commentary*, Clark, 1905), *ad loc.*

a dead body, but ours is to be a living sacrifice. The once-for-all decisive offering settles the whole direction and purpose of our lives. The repeated daily offering implements in daily living our availability for Him to use. There may be, almost certainly will be, areas of life where we are not fully realizing our complete dedication to the Lord. Here too there will need to be a rededication of ourselves, as we go on offering ourselves to Him.

Many of us meet conflicts and crises in our experience when we become conscious that we have been failing to serve the Lord as we ought. Perhaps our hearts have grown cold, or we have become spiritually proud, or undisciplined in our use of time or money, or have been neglecting prayer and have become dry and stale. Repentance and return to the Lord mean a renewal of this offering of ourselves to Him, a fresh realization of the once-for-all committal that we made at an earlier time. There is a need for us always to press on to deeper experience of the Lord, in every aspect of our lives. Self-satisfaction with spiritual progress can be a real hindrance: we need to be those who hunger and thirst for righteousness, who long for greater usefulness and effectiveness as Christians. Like Paul, we long to spend and be spent for Christ.

'Into the love of God, I pray,
        Deeper and deeper let me press . . .'[5]

I need to be sure that I am fully committed now, and to long that that committal might by its daily repetition become deeper and deeper as the days go by.

Being filled with the Spirit

But a dedicated Christian life is not only a matter of my whole-hearted giving of myself to the Lord, whom I love and who gave Himself for me, but also a matter of Him

[5] Frank Houghton, in *Christian Praise*, hymn 284.

giving Himself to me through His Holy Spirit, given to me at the time of my conversion. Thus a Christian is defined as being one who is indwelt by the Holy Spirit (Rom. 8: 9ff.); every Christian is said to be sealed by Him on believing (Eph. 1: 13) and simply to have received Him then by the hearing of faith (Gal. 3: 2). Using rather an unusual Greek word in Philippians 1: 19 (*epichorēgia*), Paul speaks of the 'help' or 'supply' of the Spirit. The same word is translated in a phrase in Ephesians 4: 16 of a ligament which serves for 'support'. There is thus in this word a wonderful idea of 'under-girding', 'strengthening', 'stiffening', 'putting backbone into', which is the Spirit's supplying of our need of strength to be the kind of Christian this book has tried to describe. Or, as Paul puts it again in the same letter, 'God is at work in you, both to will and to work for his good pleasure' (Phil. 2: 13). The fact of His indwelling and in-working needs to be appreciated, rejoiced in, and His guidance and supply of power daily appropriated.

In the Bible, being filled with the Spirit is set before us not as a single experience which we must seek, so much as a command which we must obey daily (Eph. 5: 18). The verb is a passive, present imperative, 'go on being filled by the Spirit'; that is, we are to allow the Spirit to go on filling us continuously. The command is one to appropriate continuously what the Holy Spirit gives: His power, all His fruits of love, joy and peace, all the freshness of the boisterous wind and the vitality of the living water—all this we are to appropriate, to be filled with and to overflow with.

This, then, is the conclusion of the whole matter, that if you and I want to be people who are whole-heartedly dedicated to God, who want to serve the Lord with all we have, who want to work for Him in the church and in the world, then it must be in the power and under the leadership of the Holy Spirit of God. We need to be abandoned to Him, so that He can fill us and use us for His glory.

> 'O Holy Ghost, Thy people bless,
>   Who long to feel Thy might,
> And fain would grow in holiness
>   As children of the light.

> To Thee we bring, who art the Lord,
>   Ourselves to be Thy throne;
> Let every thought, and deed, and word
>   Thy pure dominion own.'[6]

Suggestions for prayer and meditation

Am I rejoicing in being joined to the living vine, and am I bearing fruit for Him?

Am I busily engaged in Christian activity as a matter of duty or habit, without a real sense of dependence upon the Holy Spirit?

Is my Quiet Time one of arid study and dry prayer, or do I find that the Lord is teaching me His will, and that this prompts me to a warm response in prayer?

Are we trusting in meetings, organizations, methods, committees—instead of trusting more directly in the power and guidance of the Holy Spirit?

Have I made a full committal of myself to the Lord Jesus and given Him all my members, my faculties and gifts as instruments for His service?

Am I renewing this dedication day by day, and implementing my committal of myself to Christ, in practical outworking?

Am I obeying the command to go on being filled with the Holy Spirit?

[6] H. W. Baker, in *Christian Praise*, hymn 125.